Acts of Apostles

Building Faith Communities

Leonard Doohan

Resource Publications, Inc.
San Jose, California

Available SCRIPTURE FOR WORSHIP & EDUCATION Titles
Matthew
Mark
Luke
John
Acts of Apostles

Forthcoming SCRIPTURE FOR WORSHIP & EDUCATION Titles
Revelation
1 and 2 Corinthians

Editorial director: Kenneth Guentert
Managing editor: Elizabeth J. Asborno
Copyeditor and illustrator: Kathi Drolet
Front cover icon: George Collopy

© 1994 Resource Publications, Inc. No part of this book may be photocopied or otherwise reprinted, without written permission from the publisher. For permission to reprint, write to:

Reprint Department
Resource Publications, Inc.
160 E. Virginia Street #290
San Jose, CA 95112-5876

Library of Congress Cataloging in Publication Data
Doohan, Leonard.
    Acts of Apostles : building faith communities : a spiritual commentary / by Leonard Doohan.
        p.   cm. — (Scripture for worship & education)
    Includes bibliographical references and index.
    ISBN 0-89390-292-6
    1. Bible. N.T. Acts—Criticism, interpretation, etc.
I. Title. II. Series.
BS2625.2.D66   1994
226.6'06—dc20   93-47959

Printed in the United States of America

98 97 96 95 94 | 5 4 3 2 1

Scripture quotations are from the New Revised Standard Version of the Bible, copyright 1989 by the Division of Christian Education of the National Council of the Churches of Christ in the USA. Used by permission. All rights reserved.

*To Virginia and Angela
co-workers, colleagues, and friends*

Contents

Preface:
The Scripture for Worship & Education Series vii

Introduction: Transforming Christian Community . . . 1
   Pastoral Leadership
   Visioning Community
   Welcoming Everyone
   Celebrating Faith
   Imitating the Church's Great Deeds

1. The Author of Acts of Apostles 9
   Luke the Author of Acts
   Luke the Writer
   Luke the Historian and Theologian

2. Communities and Community in Acts 33
   Early Missionary Expansion
   Early Travels outside Jerusalem
   Paul's Missionary Journeys
   A Sense of Community in the Early Church

3. Luke's Purpose in Writing Acts 61
   Major Compositional Features in Acts
   Recurring Themes in Acts
   Theology of the Word

4. Images of God in Acts 87
The God of Glory
Jesus, the Living Lord
The Holy Spirit—the Father's Promise

5. Life in the Early Church 109
The Nature of the Church
Living As Church
A Worshipping Church
A Ministering Church

6. Discipleship in Acts 139
Baptized in the Name of Jesus
Followers of the Way
Prisoners in the Spirit
Witnesses to All Jesus Did

7. Living As an Easter People 161
Building Communities of Faith
Cycle A
Cycle B
Cycle C

Afterword 187

Notes 189

Resources 195

Index of Scripture References 203

Index of Authors Cited 215

Index of Subjects 217

Preface

The Scripture for Worship & Education Series

This biblical theology series is especially designed for the pastoral minister. Unlike exegetical commentaries, which provide verse-by-verse analyses, the SCRIPTURE FOR WORSHIP & EDUCATION series provides a broader examination of the context and themes of the New Testament books. The commentaries explore a biblical book's audience, purpose, key themes, understanding of Church, sense of mission and ministry. The series can be used as the basis for parish adult education programs, Scripture study groups, retreats, or personal theological and spiritual renewal.

Why Read Acts of Apostles?

Acts is a wonderful book to read for any disciple but especially for anyone involved in the ongoing renewal of parish life today. Luke's description of the life of the early Church is not only a historical portrait but also a model of the way every generation of Church should follow. Luke writes in an extraordinarily challenging

Preface: The Scripture for Worship Series

way, conveying to readers his own enthusiasm for the Lord Jesus and the Church.

Why read this particular book about Acts? Perhaps some of the following may be considered:

1. This book displays the portraits of God, Church, faith, mission, and discipleship in the early Church from one of the best single records we have of these issues. But it will not just leave you with historical records; it will challenge you to apply those issues and the implied vision to contemporary life in the Church.

2. This book describes some of the catechetical emphases that a skilled pastoral leader like Luke used in the education and spiritual formation of his community. His successful endeavor and pastorally sensitive presentations can form the basis for contemporary ministers' parish programs.

3. At a time when parishes throughout the country are engaging in all sorts of parish renewal programs, Acts is unquestionably one of the best programs of renewal in which any parish can be engaged. Why use pre-packaged programs instead of direct reflection on the New Testament challenges?

4. Luke is one of the most skillful and visionary pastoral leaders that any contemporary Christian could ever meet. He is a model of dedication to the ongoing search for faith and for ways in which faith can be practiced.

5. The Church has appropriately chosen Acts for the liturgical readings in the Easter

season. Parish leaders can find no better preparation for leading their community in post-Easter liturgical education and renewal than this volume from the Scripture for Worship Series.

6. With the Church's renewed emphasis on the Rite of Christian Initiation of Adults (RCIA), Acts and this book's commentary show that Acts can be the outline of a post-Easter mystagogia.

7. This book offers the best of modern biblical scholarship to adult Christians, with appreciation for their maturity, dedication, and vision. Christianity is a faith rooted in the original call of Jesus, not a spiritual encounter that surfaces in new ways in each generation. So disciples will find this book gives the needed knowledge of the faith upon which we all strive to base our lives.

8. This book is the result of years of teaching Acts in classes and adult education programs. As such, the author hopes it can be a good teaching tool for others. Luke deals with more issues of interest to contemporary men and women than any other writer of New Testament times. It is an astounding opportunity to enthusiastically present the challenges of Christianity in ways relevant to contemporary believers.

9. It is important for all of us, as dedicated Christians, to know about the origins of our faith. This book synthesizes the teachings of Acts, applying them to contemporary situations in our own lives.

Preface: The Scripture for Worship Series

10. Luke writes more of the New Testament than any other writer. In reading Acts we have the opportunity to study and reflect on a major part of the Scriptures that are the foundation of our faith.

Introduction

Transforming Christian Community

Pastoral Leadership

Luke is a wonderful catechist and pastoral leader. The author of Acts is an exciting person who integrates into his retelling of the stories of Jesus and the Church many interests that appeal to modern men and women: the universal call to holiness, the roles of women in the Church, an institutional commitment to social justice, collegiality, and the universal call to ministry, to mention a few. Luke wrote both the Third Gospel and Acts, the largest amount of the New Testament from a single writer. He asks many new questions of the oral traditions and give Christian interpretations for new issues with which his predecessors and even contemporaries did not deal.

Luke demonstrates a creative responsibility for the faith and approaches critical issues with insight. At a major turning point in the history of early Christianity, when the Church leaves behind its Jewish roots and becomes a world Church to spread throughout the empire, Luke reinterprets Jesus' message for new

Introduction: Transforming Christian Community

times and new conditions. Thus he provides an example for present-day communities to follow in their constant efforts to be faithful while presenting Jesus' message in ways that are relevant to changing times and cultures.

Chapter 1 focuses on Luke the author, writer, historian, and theologian. While ideas will be developed in more detail there, we can anticipate some of the ways in which Luke is an outstanding example of pastoral leadership for each of us. Luke teaches future generations as much by his own personal attitudes as he does by what he writes. Totally dedicated to Christ by a deliberate personal choice, he is not an eyewitness of Jesus' ministry nor even a companion of one of Jesus' early enthusiastic followers. Rather, his own mature faith led him to place Jesus at the center of his life and to see Christianity as a commitment that needs to permeate every aspect of life. Known as "the enthusiast for Christ," Luke adapts a Jewish-based tradition to his Gentile audience because he is convinced of the perennial relevance of Jesus' message.

We will see how Luke, whom we strive to imitate in our pastoral ministries, uses all his talents in service to the Word. He courageously incarnates the Lord's message, discerning the kernel of truth from its cultural trappings. Thus, he is able to preserve both the values of the original disciples' experience of faith and that faith's contemporary relevance to each of us today.

Some of Luke's interests are those on which we too focus today:

- the universal call to holiness
- renewal through ministry
- appreciation of the charisms of all the faithful
- commitment to community notions of the Church

- vision of authority as service
- understanding Christian institutions as collegially governed

Visioning Community

Acts is not a chronology of events in the early Church but a vision composed of what the community considered essential to its life. Luke does not list every event but describes what was typically emphasized by the early believers. This vision is not something we can pass over in our own time, for Luke insists his synthesis leaves aside occasional manifestations of faith and focuses on what is essential to the community expression of faith. In other words, we cannot ignore Luke's vision in Acts because he is telling us what we must know to successfully express our faith as a community.

Unlike Mark's community, which is undergoing persecution, Matthew's community, which is in conflict with Pharisaic Judaism, and John's community, which is struggling with whether to join the great Mother Church or remain independent, Luke's community seems to have no external pressures that challenge its faith. Luke faces a pastor's most difficult problem: How can I bring religious meaning to the lives of people who are relatively free of problems, enjoying life, comfortable, and free of persecution? Luke's solution is to call his comfortable, unchallenged readers to renewal through improving their community life and through reaching out in dedicated Christian service to others in need. Luke's vision of renewal in Acts presents community and ministry as two poles. All Christian values move around the axis of these two poles, and believers are challenged to build up their inner community life and reach out in service to others.

Introduction: Transforming Christian Community

Acts shows us how groups come together in faith, what binds them together, and what characterizes their common life in the Lord. Luke's vision of community life challenges his people to transform their lives; his vision is also remarkably challenging today as so many parishes search for a blueprint of community. While renewal programs may help, parishes could just as easily build on Luke's vision.

Luke uses the concept of spiritual journey to illustrate his vision of community. He leads his own readers, and us as well, to the desire to journey together with the Lord as an apostolic community. Acts shows us motives for wanting to belong to Christian community, forms of sharing that characterize its life, various ways believers can organize their life together, and practical ways of reaching out to evangelize others.

Luke's teachings about community, discussed in detail in chapters 2 and 5 of this book, indicate his perennial challenges to believers to build their communal expressions of faith—ideas that can easily form the basis of parish and adult renewal.

Welcoming Everyone

Luke envisions the Church as the community in which everyone can find a home. In the Gospel, he shows us Jesus, who is without a trace of discrimination. In Acts, Luke shows us Peter, the leader of the apostles, as he discovers something about God that becomes a guiding principal for the Church: God shows no partiality but treats all people equally. This spirit of openness enables the Church to reach out to the whole world, bringing Jesus' healing grace to everyone.

Luke's challenge to his readers to transform Christian community life includes the understanding that all communities of the faithful are small parts of the world-wide community of God. He shows us the expansion of a Church that learns quickly to rise above the centuries-old division between Jews and Samaritans, to overcome the stereotyping of Gentiles, to breach the artificial boundaries that former generations invented for social or religious reasons, and to dialogue with civil institutions rather than treat them as enemies.

Being open to others with the welcoming love of God is not attained without conversion. Being ready to accept the basic goodness of everyone is not something Luke encourages for social reasons but because of faith. Christianity is the religion of non-discrimination, and in Acts those Church leaders who do not perceive this are directed by God through visions to change their views. They are asked to commit themselves to a vision of universal community.

Celebrating Faith

Luke's two volumes are beautifully written and command reverence from readers. He has the skill to create an atmosphere conducive to the reception of the message he presents. When we read Acts we can easily sense the Church's enthusiasm and joy as it expanded and grew in quality of community life. As the biblical communities gather together to celebrate the achievements of the missionaries, we feel we are in their gathering, listening to the great things God has done through the Church and sharing in the joy the community feels in the successes of its delegates. Reading of God's interventions to protect the missionaries, we are drawn into the reverence and gratitude the Church expresses. Furthermore, as preachers proclaim the call to conversion "now" and "today," we cannot but respond personally to the Lord's call to us.

Introduction: Transforming Christian Community

Acts describes a celebrating community and also cultivates the same qualities in us. We find over and over again that the principal work of the people (*laos ergon,* "liturgy") is to glorify the Lord through lives and ministry that both complement and prove the authenticity of worship. We find that communities move spontaneously from discussion, ministry, and even persecution to prayer. Often, prayer moves naturally into ministry, as ministry is seen with greater clarity and urgency after prayer.

Acts gives so many examples of personal, ritual, and community prayers, it can be both challenging to and formative of our own celebrations of faith.

Imitating the Church's Great Deeds

The word "acts" in "Acts of Apostles" means the great deeds of the heroes of the early Church. Acts tells us of the many journeys that self-sacrificing believers make to spread the good news. It also shows us the great deeds of Luke himself, as one who preaches through the written Word. More than anything, Acts gives us a theology of proclamation; it details the evangelizing ministry of the Church.

The core message we receive in reading about these examples of preaching is neither about the Church's structure nor ethical teachings but rather the irruption of the divine into human history. Luke's portrait of God is exciting and challenging, and he urges believers to model their lives on God's revelation.

Luke's vision of the believing community is one of a sharing, worshiping, and ministering Church that is both local and universal. Moreover, Acts' universal call to holiness and ministry is as profoundly challenging today as it was in Luke's time. Each member of the Church—then and now—is important, for each one has a necessary role in the work of the whole community. Baptized in the name of the Lord Jesus, each disciple becomes a follower of the Way, a willing prisoner to the guidance of the Holy Spirit, and a confident witness to all Jesus did and wishes to do.

Each believer's life needs to be a celebration of the Lord's resurrection. Thus, disciples in Acts gather together to live as the Lord's Chosen People, proclaiming faith in Jesus and calling others to repentance. The faith-filled community proves its faith in action, evangelizing others and continuing Jesus' mission. The members of the community share responsibility for the good news as together they strive to bring the power of the Holy Spirit to influence every aspect of the world.

The Church reads Acts in the period after Easter.[1] While Acts covers approximately thirty years in the life of the Church, it conveys the enthusiasm of believers after the resurrection of the Lord and fosters similar responses in today's local communities of Easter people. May this book aid in drawing readers to a deeper appreciation of Luke's call in Acts—the call to rise again with the Lord to a new life as individuals of faith and as apostolic communities dedicated to extending the good news to the ends of the earth!

Chapter One

The Author of Acts of Apostles

> In the first book, Theophilus, I wrote about all that Jesus did and taught from the beginning until the day when he was taken up to heaven, after giving instructions through the Holy Spirit to the apostles whom he had chosen (Acts 1:1-2).

In these first few lines of Acts of Apostles, the author explains that he wrote another book about Jesus. Ancient manuscripts contain both the Gospel of Luke and Acts of Apostles together. Since it is unlikely that the writer of the Gospel of John also wrote the Book of Revelation, it is safe to say that Luke wrote more of the New Testament than any other writer. To write a Gospel when there already existed at least two others is surprising and might need some explaining, but to write Acts of Apostles, the only such volume in the canon of Sacred Scripture, is quite extraordinary.

But then, Luke is an extraordinary person, hailed by some as "an enthusiast for Christ" and condemned by others because they think he disrupted the traditions by introducing "early Catholicism," emphasizing structures and practices similar to modern-day Catholicism. His two-volume work, written in the best Greek of the New Testament, is the focal point of debate among the Church traditions of contemporary Christianity. Luke is the primary evangelist to address such topics as ministry, hierarchy, the role of women, authority, community, forms of faith sharing, and sacraments, to mention a few. In the fifty-two chapters of his two-volume work, Luke deals with a wide range of topics with an enthusiasm and excitement that continues to create the spirit of our liturgical year: the expectancy in the annunciation as the year begins, the joy of the shepherds and angels at Christmas, the sense of compassion the crowd experiences in the Galilean ministry, the determination felt during the journey to Jerusalem, the intoxication of the outpouring at Pentecost, and the spirit of sharing in the life of the early Church. In fact, in all his accounts, Luke creates an atmosphere conducive to the reception of the message he is presenting. Luke is a challenging proclaimer of the Good News, and perhaps in our study of his work we can catch some of his enthusiasm for Christ and his Church.

Luke the Author of Acts

Visionary of Christianity

Luke's writings show him to be a great servant to the evangelizing ministry of the early Church and also indicate his own personal dedication to the Lord. The task he undertook was enormous for those times—traveling to churches to hear about their tradition of Jesus when traveling involved so much hardship; writing fifty-two chapters of Luke-Acts when writing materials were so scarce and expensive; finding time to do this exhaustive work while providing for his basic needs—

yet he dedicated himself to a writing ministry in addition to maintaining his life and service within the local churches.

Luke gives us the basis of traditions that later develop—the local church selecting its ministers, the conveying of power through the imposition of hands, and the gathering of Church leaders for major decisions affecting the Church—and claims to document carefully everything he presents (Lk 1:3). He has great knowledge not only of the origins of the Church but also of those things early Christians considered essential to their individual and corporate calling, such as reflection on the teachings of the apostles, prayer, community, sharing, and the Eucharist. He grounds these traditions in the history of the early Church, not simply by giving a chronicle of events but by selecting those events that reflect the legacy of faith. His prime focus may have been the development of the early Church, but he also tells us how to "be Church" in succeeding generations.

In his two volumes on Jesus and the Church, Luke gives us more than past events; he also shows remarkable skill in interpreting the Lord's perennial message for different cultures and peoples. He takes a Palestinian-based tradition and translates it for a cultured Gentile audience and uses many of the literary techniques of classical Greek writers (as we will see in chapter three). The way he interprets the message shows us in turn how to use the sources and traditions of our faith. Though always respectful of his sources, he is never enslaved to them; he shows us how to catch the spirit of Scripture and relive it in changed situations.

Luke portrays great variety in the early Church. He writes of several Church structures, forms of authority, rituals, theologies, local founders and charismatic leaders. He presents them in dynamic tension, acknowledging the pluralism that he finds rather than imposing an artificial uniformity.

When Luke writes, be it in the Gospel or in Acts, he frequently presents his convictions in a pre-determined format, repeating the same ideas every time he addresses the topic. The repetition indicates his "theology" on this or that particular issue. This repetition not only makes the theologian's task easier but also makes Luke-Acts a wonderful tool or handbook for catechists.

The author of Acts' enthusiasm for the Word of God clearly permeates all his work. His theology of the Word of God is sublime and practical. The early Church's evangelization energizes missionaries with a spirit of discovery, as they proclaim the Word of God and thereby foster the expansion of the Church. It is equally clear that Luke's vision of the Church is long-term; he does not have an expectation of the immediate return of the Lord but looks forward to the future with hope and with a sense of responsibility.

The Author of Acts in the Church's Early Traditions

In the early sixties the apostle Paul, while in a prison in Rome, wrote to a personal friend called Philemon. At the end of his short letter, he added the greetings of his colleague Luke (v 24). Some of Paul's later interpreters wrote letters in Paul's name and made them look as authentic as possible. When the person who wrote the letter to the Colossians remembered that Philemon lived in Colossae, he added greetings from Luke, Paul's beloved physician (Col 4:14). In another letter written in the name of Paul, the author tells Timothy, whom he presumes knows Luke (based on Acts 16:1,10), that only Luke has remained faithful to him (2 Tim 4:11). Early Fathers of the Church also thought that Paul referred to Luke when he spoke to the Corinthians about a famous preacher (2 Cor 8:18). The manuscripts of Luke-Acts contain the name "Luke," and the early

Church quickly concluded that the author was the person mentioned in the Pauline letters.

Acts describes the great deeds of early missionaries. It is generally written in the third person singular or plural. However, after 16:10 the voice changes and the writer begins to use the first person plural, giving the impression that the author is now part of the group of traveling companions. Many commentators believe these passages are well integrated into Acts, both stylistically and theologically, and cannot easily be set aside as a separate, unconnected source. Early Church writers believed—as do many contemporary scholars—that these "we passages" indicate that the writer included himself as part of the traveling group; they presumed Luke accompanied Paul from the second missionary journey until Paul's imprisonment in Rome at the end of Acts. The early Church writers were convinced that the "we passages" easily combine with the references in the Pauline letters. They "confirm" that the Luke who authored the Third Gospel and Acts is the same Luke referred to in the Pauline letters and the same person implied in the "we passages." Presuming this connection, early Church writers from the mid-second century on generally agreed that Paul's companion Luke authored both volumes.[1] Since the early Church liked to attribute Church writings to well-known apostolic figures, thereby giving and recognizing their authority, many of the Church Fathers felt that Luke—a relatively secondary figure—must have been the actual writer, otherwise the Church would probably have attributed Acts to a better-known figure of the early Church (Bruce, *Acts*, 4). Gradually the early Church compiled the biography of the author of the Third Gospel: a doctor, secretary, companion of Paul, and someone who originated from Antioch, the great foundational and missionary city of early Christianity.[2]

The Author of Acts in Contemporary Scholarship

Most modern authors acknowledge that, based on internal evidence such as common ideas, language, and theology, the writer of Acts is the same as the author of the Third Gospel.

However, many scholars consider the author of the Third Gospel to be an anonymous Luke, unconnected with either the Luke of the New Testament letters or the companion presumed to have traveled with Paul. In fact, the connection between the author of Luke-Acts and Paul made by ancient writers was based on information from the New Testament itself, rather than on external, confirmatory proof.

Many contemporary scholars see the "we passages" in Acts as an example of a common technique in Hellenistic literature of the first century, eminently imitated by Luke. Maybe Luke did spend some time with Paul, but many contemporary writers do not think the "we passages" offer proof. These contemporary scholars of ancient literature consider that the "we passages" are a theological and literary device used in Hellenistic and Roman historiography. They think these passages are meant to give the impression of the author's direct involvement in the events, to foster the reader's confidence in the author, to give confidence in the accuracy of decisive moments in the history being described, and to involve the reader in the occurring events. Introducing the "we passages" in the narration of Paul's second journey is not unlike other writings that introduce the technique already part-way through the narrative.

The majority of contemporary scholars consider that Luke was a Gentile because of his constant interest in the Gentiles and his exclusion of anything that could be interpreted negatively by Gentiles.[3] They also point to his lack of accurate knowledge of Palestine and a lack of interest in issues exclusive to Judaism.

Of considerable interest to contemporary writers is the fact that the Paul described by Luke in Acts is notably different than the Paul who emerges from his own letters.[4] There are many inconsistencies between the two, not only of a historical nature but theological and ecclesiastical, too. Luke neither quotes from any of Paul's letters nor refers to him as an apostle. Luke presents a different theology, christology, and eschatology in Paul's sermons in Acts than Paul gives in his letters.[5] Whatever failures Paul's communities accuse him of in his letters, he does not have in Acts.[6] These differing portraits has led some (including the present writer) to conclude that Luke, who undoubtedly esteemed Paul, did not actually know the Paul of history but wrote of him as a great hero from the past—respected but no longer a vital influence in the contemporary Church life of Luke's community.[7]

Luke the Writer

Acts in the Ancient World

When Paul, the Apostle of the Gentiles, extended his ministry of evangelization through his apostolic correspondence, he used the typical letter-writing format of the ancient world (H. Doohan 6-7). When Mark wrote the first Gospel around 65-70, he developed a new form of literature. When Luke wrote his two volumes, he did not title the second since it formed part of the Gospel manuscript. Later the early Fathers of the Church began to see it as a separate book describing the life and structures of the early Church. At the end of the second century and beginning of the third, Church leaders, wanting to collect the Scriptures, placed the four Gospels together and separated Luke's second volume from his first. At that time they struggled to come up with a title. Some, such as Irenaeus, called it "Luke's witness about the apostles," and others, such as Tertullian, "Luke's commentary." Eventually, the title that seemed to best portray the content was "Acts of Apostles."

"Acts" was not a new form of literature, for it was used in the ancient world as a way of collecting stories about former heroes. "Acts" in Greek literature means "an account of great deeds." We could speak of the "Acts of Alexander the Great" or the "Acts of Hannibal." This form of writing makes no claim to be complete history. It is intended to give the reader insight into the kinds of great deeds that characterized or typified the leader described. Luke, who knew well the language and culture of the Hellenistic world as well as the historical and literary methods of its writers, chose this form of literature for his second volume.

The acts described in this second volume are the great deeds of apostles. Today we generally say, "The Acts of the Apostles," but there is no definite article "the" in the title in Greek. Moreover, the book does not speak about the apostles as if it were a description of the great deeds of the Twelve. In fact, apart from a single mention of the Twelve (Acts 1:13), the book only refers to Peter, except for a few references to John when he accompanies Peter (3:1; 4:1,13; 8:14-17,25). It mentions Stephen and Philip, both deacons; James the brother of the Lord and leader of the Jerusalem Church (but not an apostle); Paul; Barnabas; Dorcas; John Mark and his mother, Mary; Acquila and his wife, Priscilla; Apollos; Lydia; and Silas—great figures but not listed among the Twelve.

The acts described in this book are the great deeds of apostolic individuals whose self-dedication to the Lord and commitment to the ministry of the Church are examples for believers of all generations. Only one,

Peter, belonged to the Twelve. Paul was specially chosen by the Lord. Others are well-known members of the early Church's missionary enterprise, and still others are unknown and even unnamed but nonetheless great contributors to the life and development of the Church. It is the great deeds of the named and unnamed about which Luke has chosen to write.

Other "Acts" from the Christian Era

There are several books of "Acts" among the apocryphal writings (those writings on Christian themes that are not part of the New Testament) of the early Church. Among them is Acts of Peter, written around the year 200. This book tells the story of Peter's departure from Rome because of persecution and his encounter with Jesus, who enters Rome to take Peter's place. Acts of Andrew, also from around 200, describes among other things Andrew's martyrdom on an X-shaped cross. Acts of Thomas presents the great missionary work of the apostle to India. There are also Acts of John, Philip, and Paul. None of these writings became part of the canon of Scripture; indeed, they affirm heresies such as encratism, a teaching against the sexual life of the married—preachers in these Acts advise wives to leave their husbands. These apocryphal Acts also contain exaggerations contrary to the faith of the early Church (for example, an unhealthy exaggeration of the miraculous).

An "Acts," then, was a common form of literature in the ancient world. It was used by Luke and was imitated by other Christian writers. Luke's book alone was accepted into the canon of Scripture. Its canonicity was firmly established by 160-180 CE. (It was probably considered canonical several decades earlier. Once Luke's Gospel was accepted, Acts was probably accepted along with it.) Several early Church documents—the writings of Clement of Rome, Ignatius of

Antioch, and Polycarp of Smyrna—have quotations similar to those in Acts; while these writers do not quote Acts, the references indicate that Acts contains a spirit similar to that of the sub-apostolic age.

Sources in Acts

Contemporary commentators generally agree that Luke uses sources in composing the Third Gospel. These sources include Mark (which accounts for a quarter of Luke); the "Q" source, material common to Matthew and Luke but not found in Mark (which accounts for another quarter of Luke); and a third source, exclusive to him, called "L." We know that Luke uses Mark with reverence, yet he only uses fifty percent of his ideas and only twenty-five percent of his vocabulary. Luke uses his sources more critically than does Matthew, who copies accurately 600 out of 661 verses in Mark. We have already seen that whether Luke knew Paul or not, he did not repeat his theological positions. Luke either ignored them or substantially changed them to suit new needs. Our writer Luke is not a slave to his sources; he stamps all his sources with his own personal style and skillfully molds them into a unified work.

It is easy to identify possible sources of the Third Gospel because we have four Gospels to compare. Since the three Synoptic Gospels—Matthew, Mark, and Luke—all have material in common, it is possible to identify shared sources and note the changes introduced by each of the writers. We have no such good fortune regarding Acts, because we have no other canonical Acts with which to compare Luke's. However we can presume that if he used sources, he probably treated them in the same way he treated his sources for the Third Gospel.[8]

Some Lukan scholars have pointed out that Acts is composed of stories that deal with significant people:

Peter, James, Philip, Paul, and a possible traveling companion of Paul. They think each of these people could be one of Luke's sources. Others suggest that these famous individuals are each identified with a special place; these scholars combine people and places into a series of possible sources: a Jerusalem (Mark) source, a Caesarean (Philip) source, an Antiochean (Luke) source, and a Samaritan (Stephen) source.

In the early part of Acts, there seem to be two versions of the ascension story, two strands in the Pentecost story, two versions of the account of Stephen's martyrdom, three versions of Peter's visit to Cornelius, and two approaches to the Council in Jerusalem.[9] In the section of Acts that deals with Paul, some writers see three possible sources interwoven into the narrative: the "we" source, a speech source, and an itinerary source (which itself contains a sea voyage source). These double or parallel forms of the tradition, together with the integration of various literary forms into the whole, persuade several commentators to think that Luke did use sources for Acts even if they are not as easily identifiable as those in his Gospel. As in the Gospel, Luke reworked his material thoroughly, but some writers feel that traces of separate sources are still visible.

Stylistic Features in Acts

Acts is not a simple recollection of what happened; it is Luke's presentation of material that communicates a vision of Church. He gives a vision of the early Church that he thinks will motivate the future Church. He is more personally involved in the composition of Acts than he is in the Gospel.

Luke is generally faithful to his sources, respecting them and letting them speak for themselves. He does, however, give them each his personal stamp—his vision, aims, and interests as an author and as a theologian. He does not radically modify them, otherwise why would he use them? He shows great openness and flexibility in adapting a Jewish-based tradition for a Gentile world. He generally polishes the style of the sources, in places changing the material for greater clarity or adapting them to the cultural differences of his audience.[10] He uses the Jewish Scriptures not only for theological reasons but also to create the specific style or atmosphere that he thinks could benefit a passage. In places, he introduces reflections of rabbis without disturbing the flow of the passage for non-Jews while bringing significant links for those Jews who see the emphases.

Luke has an excellent knowledge of Greek, whether classical, septuagintal, or *koiné*, and his vocabulary is as extensive as most classical Greek writers. He adapts the methods and literary forms of the Gentile world that he knows so well. The prefaces, letters, travelogues, philosophical discussions, and speeches in Acts were common literary forms in the Greco-Roman world.[11] Furthermore, Luke modifies his source material to fit it into the structures and strategy that he gives his two volumes. For example, he balances some narratives in Acts with similar stories in his Gospel. We read of the baptisms of Jesus and the Church (Lk 3:21-22; Acts 2:1-4), the inaugural speeches of Jesus and Peter (Lk 4:14-20; Acts 2:14-41), and the cures wrought by Jesus and by disciples (Lk 5:17-20; Acts 9:32-35). Luke wants to show that the power that was alive in Jesus is now present in the early Church. In Acts he parallels stories of Peter with stories about Paul to show that what Peter did for the Jews Paul did for the Gentiles (Acts 2:14-41 and 13:16-41; 3:1-10 and 14:8-10; 5:15-16 and 19:11-12). Through these and other techniques, Luke unifies the Gospel with Acts and connects various parts within Acts.

Thus, while Luke presents his work in a series of theological and literary patterns that are not always easy to see, this usage may well indicate that his community was well aware of fixed forms of the tradition because of their own retelling of episodes in their community gatherings.

Luke the Historian and Theologian

Historian of the Ancient World

It is possible to incorporate accurate historical data into a work even when history is not the work's principal concern. Consequently, even if Luke's principal concern is theological and evangelical, we cannot immediately conclude that he is historically unreliable. Some commentators have criticized Luke's lack of historical reliability because he freely adapts and modifies his sources, he tends to fit stories into predetermined structures, he is often chronologically inaccurate in comparison with other New Testament writers, and finally, because he has a fondness for introducing, and at times exaggerating, the miraculous. After reading Acts, many other writers still express the conviction that Luke's primary goal is to present the history of the early Church.

We cannot judge Luke by our contemporary understanding of history. While historians may see their role as being detached observers of past events, we are often unpersuaded that historians give us objective facts but generally assume that they give us their interpretation of the facts. In the ancient world, whether Greek, Roman, or Jewish, rulers often hired historians to write about them. More particularly, historians and biographers in Luke's time presented their work within a philosophy or theology of history. For example, the

Romans told stories of their emperors against the backdrop of the activities of their gods. They were theologians precisely because they were historians or biographers. Luke, then, is also a theologian precisely because he is a first-century historian.

Luke uses history to unfold progressively the rooted faith of the early Church. He can delete the negative side of events and people—excluding from Acts, for example, some of Peter's negative traits evidenced in the Gospel. Luke sees himself as one responsible for handing on the faith, a steward of the tradition, and so detailed biographical information is not his concern. Nor is it his intention to write history for its own sake. Rather he writes to assure believers of the rootedness of their faith and to remind them of the essential elements of that faith.

Luke writes to remind Christians that their salvation has been revealed in foundational events of the past, events that not only give assurance to believers but also direction for the future. These events are not chosen simply because they happened and he wants to chronicle them; he selects events that both model and challenge the faith of successive generations. Luke is a historian precisely because he is a theologian.

Christian Origins

Acts stresses Paul's expected martyrdom on three occasions (20:22-23; 21:4-5,11) just as the Gospel does the Lord's death (9:22,44; 18:31-32). Acts ends before Paul's trial and death and makes no mention of them. Prior to the development of a critical approach to the Christian Scriptures in the seventeenth century, it was common to presume that Luke wrote Acts before the year 64 CE because that date is the earliest possible one for the death of Paul. Moreover, Paul plays an important role in Acts, yet there is no reference in Acts to any of his letters. It is thought this could be because Paul was prominent in the early period up to about the 70s but not after the turn of the century, and his letters were not collected until later.

Acts is written to a Roman official, seemingly to ask him to support Christianity in its debates with the empire, yet Nero withdrew all of Christianity's privileges by the year 64. Some of Luke's themes, such as the admission of Gentiles into the Church, seem only appropriate in the 60s and not relevant after the fall of Jerusalem in 70 CE. Some writers, therefore, suggest Acts was written around 64, and the Gospel around 61.[12]

Other Lukan scholars offer a later date for the writing of Acts, believing that it is the result of a dialectical development in the early Church. For them Acts is the result of a prolonged interaction between pro-Jewish and anti-Jewish tendencies in the churches under James' or Paul's leadership. Some writers in favor of a late date for Acts believe that it gives the impression of looking back over an extended period of the Church's life, searching for roots. Some of these writers think Acts fits best with the apologists around 115; others think it fits after Marcion's attempt to formulate a canon—around 125 or later. The latest date suggested for the composition of Acts is around 130.[13]

However, most commentators date the writing of Luke-Acts between 80-90. These commentators think an earlier date is implausible because Luke's Gospel uses Mark, which is generally dated around 65-70.[14] While the earlier date is supported by tradition, the later date has never gained much support.

The fact that Luke says he is not an eyewitness, and probably not a minister of the Word but a compiler of the tradition (Lk 1:2), suggests his work is not early. Moreover, the kind of Church envisioned by Acts is still in a phase of development institutionally, liturgically, ministerially, and doctrinally. The writing cannot be late, for by the turn of the century much has been sorted out, and the Church has figures like Polycarp and Ignatius of Antioch. Their writings indicate the Church is no longer in a phase of development as Luke describes it; thus they postdate Luke's work.

Luke writes the Third Gospel and Acts around 80-90 for a cultured and sophisticated audience. He presents a Church that already has structures but has not yet arrived at any kind of unified vision. It has a variety of structures, beliefs, leadership roles, and visions of ministry. However, this Church is already world-minded; it reaches out to the borders of the empire, spreading the Word of Jesus the Lord. It has decided that Jesus' return will not be immediate, and in the intervening time it decides to dedicate itself to social justice and dialogue with the State. Luke's audience is basking in the comfort of a peaceful society and already needs renewal. He challenges believers to think of their roots and the implications of Jesus' original call for their contemporary life of faith.

Theologian and Pastoral Leader

In the Gospel of Luke, Jesus says something that Luke could well have made his motto: "I came to bring a fire to the earth, and how I wish it were already kindled!" (12:49). Harnack called Luke "an enthusiast for Christ," and Renan said that Luke's writings were the most beautiful book in the world. The author of the Third Gospel and Acts—which comprise more than a quarter of the New Testament—is a great historian, standing in line with the great classical historians, such as Thucydides, as well as with the great historians of the Jewish Scriptures. He respects those who have gone before him, but his interest is the Church and its new questions and new needs.

While we have seen that Luke is not a historian like modern historians, neither is he a theologian like modern theologians. With faith he goes back to the sources and searches for the consensus of the faithful. Clearly he has more of the oral traditions available to him than did his hero Paul, which may account for some of their differences. Luke's motivation in selecting his material is determined by his inspired fidelity to oral tradition. Discerning what is essential, he builds upon the truths of the tradition, even though he may show these truths in events that may not, and did not need to, have happened.

Luke is part of the evolution of the Church's tradition, charism, and teachings. Had he simply repeated everything he knew from tradition, he would merely have told us what Christianity was like two thousand years ago. By being ready to change, interpret, and reinterpret, he reminds Christians of all generations that they too are part of a chain of tradition, and they too must take their inspiration from the sources but give it new life in succeeding generations. Luke does not just offer a methodology for responsible pastoral action; he gives a spirituality for pastoral leadership.

The author of Acts is a model for Christians of all generations because he clings to the sources of his faith but is not enslaved to any formulations of faith (e.g., he takes the basic Gospel message but does not bind himself to Mark's formulation of it; he takes Paul's missionary vision but adapts it to a more urban world). Luke is convinced that the message of the Lord can be proclaimed to new cultures with freshness, vitality, and relevance. Seeking always to verify his teachings in the message of the Lord, he is never satisfied until he has interpreted that message for changed circumstances.

Whether Luke knew any of the apostolic figures is not all that clear, and critics argue as to whether they can see traces of Paul, Peter, James, Philip, or Mark in Luke's writings. Perhaps that is the way it should be—faith is not slavish attachment to the past but the willingness to change what is secondary in that past so that faith becomes relevant to the present.

Luke centers his message on the person Jesus and not on a series of abstract truths. Religions quickly get cluttered with legalism, gurus, programmed rituals, top-heavy authority structures, popular piety and devotions. Luke cuts through the superficial—such as the positions held by believers who thought it was necessary to become a Jew before becoming a Christian or those who insisted on adopting Jewish laws of purity as part of Christianity—and gets to the heart of the early traditions, re-presenting them to us in all their freshness.

Trends in Lukan Studies

Scholars refer to the period prior to the seventeenth century as the pre-critical period, since it precedes the developments of scientific methods in approaching historical and literary documents. During that period it was presumed that the author of Acts was the secretary companion of Paul, traveling with him from the time of the second missionary journey until Paul's death. In fact, when Paul told the Romans that he wanted to share his "gospel" with them (Rom 16:25), the Fathers of the Church understood that he was referring to the Third Gospel.

When critical methods were applied to the study of the Scriptures, using books like R. Simon's *A critical history of the texts of the New Testament,* readers began to identify inconsistencies in the texts that had previously gone unnoticed. Non-Christian scholars suggested that the New Testament, the Gospels in particular, were creative writings composed to support one tendency or another in the early Church. These scholars, known as tendency critics, claimed that Luke was historically unreliable because his work was biased.

Luke's bias, they claimed, was to establish a compromise between Peter and Paul in Acts.

Christian scholars such as Wescott, Lightfoot, Hort, and Ramsay reacted to these challenges by providing the scholarly community with accurate Greek texts, reliable contemporary history, and even archaeological evidence as bases for further discussion. Then others proposed that the documents were not creative writings distinct from each other but accurate ones because they used similar sources that could be seen to reflect common traditions of the early Church. Some, including Streeter, offered the two-source and then the four-source hypotheses as explanations for the interrelationship of the Gospels.

Luke is such a fine writer that some commentators see him as a storyteller who collected, selected and then arranged his material into a literary masterpiece at the service of faith. Martin Dibelius did much to emphasize this view, as did Rudolf Bultmann. These, along with other scholars, are among the first "form critics."[15]

Since the 1950s, the scholarly focus has been to view Luke as a major theologian of the early Church, someone who composed and structured his work to portray a particular theological emphasis. During the 1950s, Luke-Acts became "the storm center of New Testament scholarship" (van Unnik). Some scholars suggested Luke wrote his two volumes to legitimize a particular form of Church structure—a structure that resembled an early form of Roman Catholicism. Such writers claim that although this Church structure did not exist in Jesus' time, Luke makes it look as if it started with Jesus and thus legitimizes its presence in his own Church. These writers, among whom is Ernst Käsemann, condemned this "early catholicism" of Luke. Others saw a different theological emphasis; they believed that Luke wrote his two volumes to reinterpret the second coming, to assure believers that the end would not be soon, and to challenge them to Christian living in the time of waiting. Still other writers offered a selection of theological or evangelical emphases that they believe motivated Luke to write (L. Doohan, *Luke*, 155-172).

Writings on Luke-Acts frequently originated in Germany and Britain, whose scholars have remained divided on the approach to Luke-Acts for over a hundred years. German scholars, who are credited with a new look in Lukan studies, typically have been more liberal and given greater emphasis to Luke as a theologian. Notable among the German scholars are Hans Conzelmann, the scholar generally credited with giving a new impetus to Lukan studies, and Ernst Haenchen, who provided one of the greatest commentaries on Acts available.

In comparison British scholars have been more conservative and stressed Luke's contribution as a historian. F. F. Bruce's book on Acts is outstanding, as is the work on the theology of Luke-Acts by I. Howard Marshall. Modern readers need to read both sides and dialogue between them, possibly reading Ernst Haenchen and Hans Conzelmann on the one hand, and F. F. Bruce and I. Howard Marshall on the other.

The best scholarly presentation available from a contemporary Roman Catholic scholar is the work of Joseph Fitzmyer.[16]

Formation through Liturgy

Before any Christian Scriptures were written down, oral traditions circulated for 30-60 years. Stories were told and retold in educational, formational, and liturgical contexts. By the time episodes appear in our Scriptures, they are no longer in their primitive, raw state but have been adapted and interpreted according to communities' needs. When Luke presented Acts to his community, it is likely that his people had heard most of the stories before; the only new thing about Acts would have been the way in which Luke combined materials.

Luke is a great visionary of early Christianity. He seeks to discover the roots of our tradition and the perennial challenges they contain. However, he is only interested in going back to the sources in order to let them challenge contemporary situations. Thus, he interprets and applies the Word of the Lord, making it "spirit and life" in changing times.

Luke has a practical approach to faith and encourages readers to commit themselves to great deeds, to "acts," in their pursuit of ongoing fidelity. He is a pastoral leader who can discern between the little traditions and the great Tradition of the faith. He gives us a solid foundation of core values, values that were consistently practiced in the early Church.

Luke balances the development of the institutional Church with the development of the call of each disciple as he or she responds to the universal call to holiness, ministry, and responsibility. As we read his work during the liturgical year, we will discover that he seems to be proclaiming the message to every individual in the community.

Luke uses all his skills in the proclamation of the Word. He uses methods and stylistic features that contemporary ministers could well imitate. He creates an atmosphere conducive to the reception of faith and repeats key themes with the skill of a trained catechist.

Luke teaches us as much by the kind of believer he is as by the writings he gives us. As we bring his stories to our liturgies, we try to be visionaries who appreciate the original call of Jesus and also apply it. We dedicate ourselves not only to informing our communities but also to forming and transforming them. Like Luke, we seek to use all our talents in the service of the good news by calling everyone to an awareness of the responsibilities of faith.

For Personal and Group Reflection

1. Are you, like Luke, both faithful to early Church traditions and faithful to the call to interpret them anew for each generation? Do you feel responsible for the growth of faith in your parish?

2. As a Christian minister, do you, like Luke, give the whole of your life to Jesus' mission?

3. Do you imitate Luke's editorial skill, creating an appropriate spirit and atmosphere for each part of the Gospel message as it reappears in the liturgical year?

4. Luke wrote of the great hero Paul but was also ready to let go of any attachment to Paul's formulation of faith. Are you overly influenced by one religious guru or another, or do you take personal responsibility for bringing out the message in your environment?

5. Luke's theology of the Word is sublime and practical. Can you both preserve respect for the Word and show that respect by making practical contemporary applications of the Word's perennial call?

6. If you were to rewrite the "Acts" of a contemporary religious leader, whom would you choose and why? Could other individuals write your "Acts?" What would they emphasize?

7. Luke searched for the consensus of the faithful alive in his time. Do you seek

consensus in the faith-filled expressions of contemporary believers?

8. Luke is thought of as "the enthusiast for Christ." Is that an appropriate way to describe yourself?

9. Luke is both theologian and pastoral leader. Is your involvement in ministry grounded in ongoing religious education?

10. How can you use Luke as a guide in the post-Easter formation of the parish community?

Chapter Two

Communities and Community in Acts

> But you will receive power when the Holy Spirit has come upon you; and you will be my witnesses in Jerusalem, in all Judea and Samaria, and to the ends of the earth (Acts 1:8).

In Acts Luke tells us that after his resurrection Jesus spent forty days with the apostles, instructing them about the kingdom of God. The Lord told his followers to stay in Jerusalem to await the coming of the Holy Spirit. Luke presents this coming as the baptism of the Church, parallel to Jesus' baptism at the beginning of the Gospel.

In both the Third Gospel and Acts, the coming of the Holy Spirit is linked with an anointing for mission (Lk 4:18; Acts 10:38). Moreover, in the passage at the head of the chapter (1:8), Acts gives the apostles a plan of action for their mission: to systematically expand from Jerusalem, through Judea and Samaria to the ends of the earth. Luke, whose concern is to show the Church as faithful to the Lord's commission, develops Acts according to the missionary expansion outlined in 1:8.

After Jesus' ascension, the disciples gathered in the upper room, spending their time in prayer, as they waited for the promise of the Lord. Luke inserts a story about the election of Matthias so that the Church can reconstitute the symbolic number of twelve leaders before the formal baptism of the Church at Pentecost. The outpouring of the Spirit gives impetus to the disciples' participation in the Lord's evangelizing ministry, just as it did for Elijah in relation to Elisha (2 Kings 2:7-13) and the seventy elders in relation to Moses (Num 11:24-30). With the gift of the Holy Spirit, the apostles immediately began preaching the good news and, inspired with boldness, were able to extend this ministry and accept all the suffering and persecution that accompanied it. Gradually, through their fearless efforts, the Word was spread and communities of believers established throughout the known world.

Early Missionary Expansion

Initial Developments in Jerusalem

Modern Jerusalem traces its origin to the City of David, a small section in the southeast corner of Jerusalem. David expanded the city and planned to build a temple. According to the Law, sacrifices to Yahweh were to be offered in only one place (Deut 12:2-5). King David's plans did not materialize, and it was Solomon who built the Temple (1 Chron 28:3-7). It took seven years to complete it (1 Kings 6:37-38). This First Temple contained the Ark of the Covenant; the Holy of Holies was revered as the place where the glory of God dwelt (Ex 25:22; Heb 9:3). This magnificent building, destroyed by the Babylonians in 587 BCE, was later replaced by a less elaborate version in 515 BCE; this Second Temple was replaced by the Temple of Herod the Great, built as an attempt by Herod to gain the support of the Jewish leaders, since Herod himself was not a Jew. Herod's construction began in 19 BCE and was completed in 64 CE, just six years before it was totally destroyed by the Roman armies. Herod's Temple is the one that existed in Jesus' time. The Temple was the center of the people's lives (Isa 2:1-5) and the place of the manifestation of God's holiness (Isa 6:1-3). However, Jeremiah warned against false security in the Temple (Jer 7:1-15) and, along with other prophets, foretold its destruction (Jer 26:1-6; Mic 3:12).

Although in Mark's Gospel the disciples return to Galilee after the death of Jesus, in Luke they remain in Jerusalem. The Chosen People believed that it was Jerusalem from which salvation was to be attained (Isa 2:2-4; 40:9-11; Zech 8:20-23). Throughout his Gospel Luke highlights Jerusalem and the Temple, for Jerusalem, the Holy City, was the place from which redemption was thought to come. From the end of the Galilean ministry, Jesus "set his face to go to Jerusalem" (Lk 9:51). Throughout Jesus' final journey, Luke reminds his readers that Jesus' goal is the Holy City (Lk 10:1,38; 13:22,33). However, Jerusalem rejected the Lord it had been expecting and became an image of those who reject opportunities for salvation. In Luke's Gospel, the disciples wait in Jerusalem, even though they still have false expectations of an earthly restoration of the kingdom (Lk 24:21; Acts 1:6). As Jesus promised, the gift of the Holy Spirit fills the disciples with courage and vision, and they initiate the missionary expansion of the Church.

The Church's response to the outpouring of the Holy Spirit is the same as Jesus' own (Lk 4:18-30); the Church begins to preach the saving grace of God. Moreover, "those who welcomed his message were baptized, and that day about three thousand persons were added" (Acts 2:41); thus the first act of expansion takes place in Jerusalem. Peter continues the work of evangelization

Communities and Community in Acts

Jerusalem in the Time of the Early Church

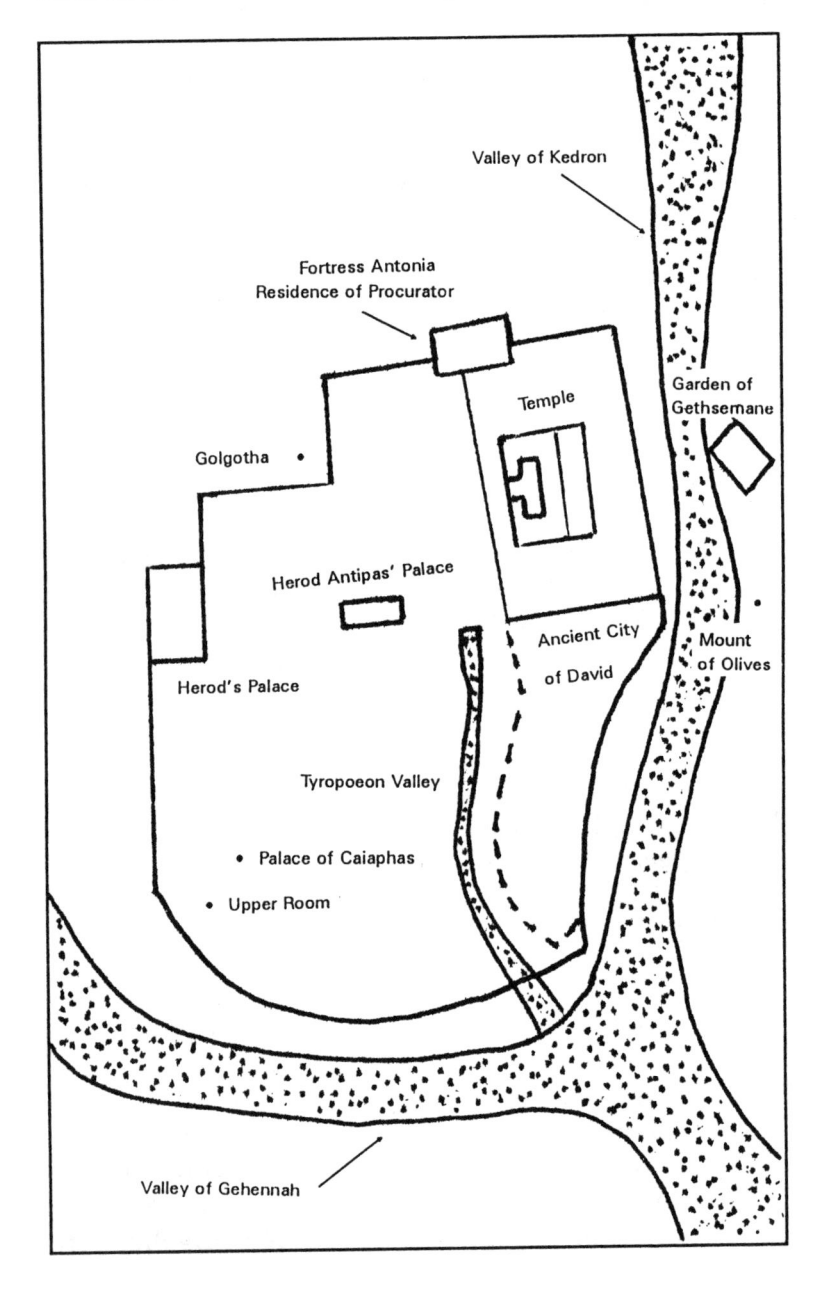

by curing a lame man at the Beautiful gate of the Temple and preaching to the people who were awestruck by the miracle. Before Peter finishes speaking, the temple guards lead him and his companion John to the Sanhedrin. Instead of listening in silence to the reprimand the Jewish leaders intend to give them, the two apostles use the occasion to preach the good news of Jesus Christ again. Returning to the Christian community to celebrate the new opportunity to preach, all pray in gratitude and ask for the gift of boldness in preaching the message (Acts 4:23-31).

In Acts, the communities of Christians in Jerusalem are united, listening to the apostles' teachings, celebrating the Lord's Supper in each other's homes, sharing their material goods, and going daily to the Temple to pray (Acts 2:42-47; 4:32-35). As their numbers grow, problems arise, both internal—such as that between Peter and two disciples, Ananias and his wife, Sapphira (Acts 5:1-11)—and external—such as the persecution by the Sanhedrin (Acts 5:17-18; 9:1-2). Despite these problems, the community's sense of commitment endures as they share the Word in the Temple and in each other's homes.

Christian Community in Jerusalem

The Christian community in Acts quickly increases in numbers: "And day by day the Lord added to their number those who were being saved" (Acts 2:47). Many accept the call of God through the preaching of the apostles on the day of Pentecost and Luke can say, "So those who welcomed his message were baptized, and that day about three thousand persons were added" (Acts 2:41). Within a short period he can again say, "Yet more than ever believers were added to the Lord, great numbers of both men and women" (Acts 5:14). By his presentation of this swift expansion, Luke shows his conviction that the growth of the Church is according to the will of God. From the time of the ascension, the believers were profoundly aware that they were a special group (Acts 1:13-14; 2:42-47; 5:12-13,42), saved in the name of the Lord (Acts 2:21; 4:12). Salvation was indeed found in Jerusalem, but not in the way they expected. Salvation was found in the new community built on the new Twelve patriarchs; it was attained by those who repented, believed in Jesus, received baptism, and were blessed with the gift of the Holy Spirit (Acts 2:38). Luke presents Pentecost and the subsequent appearances of the Holy Spirit as creation accounts. He sees the birth of the Church as a new creation through the gift of the Holy Spirit. This new life also has its new Adam and Eve—Ananias and Sapphira—who fail to live out the new life God brings (Acts 5:1-11).

At first, the most important structure of the Church in Acts is the twelve apostles, who serve as the pillars of the Church at Pentecost (Acts 2:14). These Twelve later appoint the seven deacons (Acts 6:1-6). After appointing the deacons, the Twelve then disappear from the scene. Though "the apostles" are mentioned twenty times, it is not clear if these references apply to the Twelve or to a larger number that exercised authority at that time as a group of elders (Acts 1:23; 11:1-18; 15:2). The Twelve serve as the foundation of the new community and as authentic links and witnesses to the historical Jesus. The seven deacons were appointed by the Twelve to extend their service to the needy, but these seven key figures also disappear from the Jerusalem scene. The key leader in the early period is Peter. The first in the list of the Eleven (Acts 1:13), he suggests that the community elect a replacement for Judas (Acts 1:15-26) and is the Church's great preacher (Acts 2:14-36; 3:12-26; 10:34-43). He becomes spokesperson before Jewish authorities (Acts 4:8-12; 5:29-32), emerges as a person of authority (Acts 5:1-11; 15:7-11), and is the object of special divine protection (Acts 5:17-21; 10:9-48;

12:6-11). Peter is the recognized leader and inaugurates the Church's mission to the Gentiles (Acts 10:1-11:18). He departs Jerusalem after his miraculous release from prison (Acts 12:17), leaving James in charge (Acts 12:17; 21:18).

Luke sees conversion as a process worked out in the heart of the Church. The Jerusalem community prays together (Acts 1:14,24-25; 2:42-45; 4:32-35); it shares life (4:32), meals (Acts 2:46-47), faith (Acts 4:20), and material goods (Acts 2:44-45; 4:32-35), and it lives in an atmosphere of joy (Lk 24:52). Although there are signs of early persecution, the Twelve continue to preach the Word: "they rejoiced that they were considered worthy to suffer dishonor for the sake of the name. And every day in the Temple and at home they did not cease to teach and proclaim Jesus as the Messiah" (Acts 5:41-42).

Early Travels outside Jerusalem

The Missions of Philip and Peter

The early Church develops, people hold the Christian community in high esteem, and the Lord steadily adds to their numbers (Acts 5:13-14). Church leaders, encountering their first internal community problem, designate seven Hellenistic deacons to assist in responding to the daily social needs of the community (Acts 6:1-6). The story in Jerusalem is one of constant success: "The word of God continued to spread; the number of the disciples increased greatly in Jerusalem, and a great many of the priests became obedient to the faith" (Acts 6:7). Stephen, one of the seven deacons appointed to respond to the social needs of the community, becomes a great preacher instead and voices the community's theological differences about the importance of Jerusalem and the leadership of the Jews

Travels of Peter and Philip

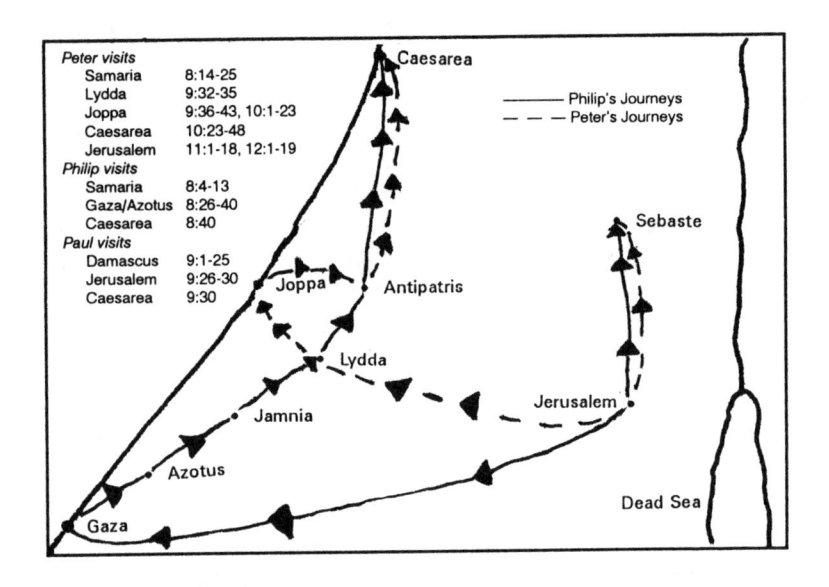

Peter visits
Samaria 8:14-25
Lydda 9:32-35
Joppa 9:36-43, 10:1-23
Caesarea 10:23-48
Jerusalem 11:1-18, 12:1-19
Philip visits
Samaria 8:4-13
Gaza/Azotus 8:26-40
Caesarea 8:40
Paul visits
Damascus 9:1-25
Jerusalem 9:26-30
Caesarea 9:30

———— Philip's Journeys
— — — Peter's Journeys

Locations: Caesarea, Sebaste, Joppa, Antipatris, Lydda, Jerusalem, Jamnia, Azotus, Gaza, Dead Sea

(Acts 7:1-53). As a result of his open opposition, Stephen is put to death (Acts 7:55-60). The resulting persecution led to the missionary expansion of the Church (Acts 8:1; 11:18-19).

Another deacon, Philip, is the first to begin the Church's evangelizing work outside of Jerusalem. He visits Samaria, where he preaches, works miracles, exorcises demons and cures the ill (Acts 8:4-13). For Luke, Philip's journey is not only geographical but theological too. Luke skillfully moves his community toward a new attitude toward the Samaritans. Acceptance of the Samaritans "must have been a progressive step which the early Christians found difficult to embrace" (Cassidy and Scharper 92-93). By this journey Luke gradually moves the reader to understand that the Gospel is moving away from Jerusalem toward the Gentile world. (The Samaritans were historically connected to the Jews but were ostracized and despised by them.) They received Philip's preaching with great joy.

With the help of missions such as Philip's, the early Church in Acts grows in its self-understanding. Those people who accept the Word and are converted to Christ receive baptism and the gift of the Holy Spirit. Sometimes baptism comes first, sometimes the Spirit comes first, but the leaders soon learn that both go together. Thus, once the Samaritans receive baptism, the apostles in Jerusalem send Peter and John to lay hands on them to receive the gift of the Holy Spirit (Acts 8:14-17). During their return journey, Peter and John continue to preach to the Samaritans—both expanding the Church and consolidating its break from Judaism.

Philip continues his travels to spread the Word, going to Gaza, Azotus, and as far as Caesarea—a journey of over 130 miles. On this journey he baptizes an Ethiopian, who, since he is not referred to as a Jew but is studying Judaism, is generally presumed to be a proselyte. Through this conversion, Luke continues to illustrate the Gospel's move away from Judaism. Luke first describes the conversion of a Samaritan, someone with Jewish heritage, and then describes the conversion of someone who is interested in Judaism but is not yet a Jew. Moreover, Luke shows that Philip's work is directed by God, whose angel advises him and whose Spirit leads him (Acts 8:26,39). Luke ends each conversion by stating that the newly baptized believer rejoices (Acts 8:8,39), for that is part of Luke's theology of conversion—self-dedication to the Lord always results in inner joy.

The early Church continues to grow: "Meanwhile the church throughout Judea, Galilee, and Samaria had peace and was built up. Living in the fear of the Lord and in the comfort of the Holy Spirit, it increased in numbers" (Acts 9:31). Luke deliberately uses this refrain to give the impression of constant growth in the Church, thereby encouraging believers and stressing God's guidance of the early Church. Peter continues to travel and visits many places including Lydda and Joppa, where he works miracles similar to those that Jesus worked: the healing of a paralytic and the raising from the dead of a woman. This paralleling of Peter's miraculous activity with Jesus' is not by chance; Luke wishes to show us that the power that was alive in Jesus is now in Peter for the sake of the Church.

While Peter is in Joppa, the Lord guides him through a vision to understand that the Gentiles are to be admitted to the Church. After the vision Peter sets out for Caesarea, where he witnesses the Holy Spirit's descent on the household of the Roman centurion Cornelius. Although a Gentile, Cornelius was not typical of Gentiles, for he was devout, God-fearing, prayerful, and supportive of Jewish causes. Here we see Luke continuing to move us step by step, in a non-threatening way from Judaism to the Gentiles.

While the early Church extended its missionary enterprises throughout Judea and Samaria, there were missionaries who went even further. For example, there was already a Christian community in Damascus by the time Paul arrived (Acts 9:10); Paul, after his conversion, was able to spend time with them (Acts 9:1-25). Following a brief visit to Jerusalem and Caesarea, Paul went off to Tarsus to continue his proclamation of the Word (Acts 9:30). Other missionaries traveled as far as Phoenicia, Cyprus, and Antioch (Acts 11:19). Barnabas and Paul worked together in Tarsus and Antioch (Acts 11:25-26,30; 12:24-25).

Paul's Missionary Journeys

First Missionary Journey

Luke's portrait of Paul is often different than the portrait that emerges from Paul's letters, but the general picture of his missionary journeys is correct. Paul's letters either confirm Luke's presentation or modify it in places. Paul's four major journeys span approximately sixteen years, from 46-62 CE. A detailed chronology is not possible, but a few significant events can be dated: the Jerusalem Council around 49, the proconsulship of Gallio in 52, possibly the procuratorships of Felix from 52-59 and Festus around 60-62.

Paul's first missionary journey takes place between 46-49 CE, and Luke describes it in Acts 13:1-14:28. Prior to this journey Paul preaches in Damascus, Jerusalem, Caesarea, and Tarsus, first working with Barnabas and then with Mark. After his conversion Paul spends about twelve years preaching the Gospel. We know little about this time Paul spent, but we can guess he probably spent it preaching to the Gentiles in the desert area of Perea (Gal 1:17). Once Barnabas introduces Paul to the Jerusalem Church, he becomes better known, and once Paul takes up residence in Antioch, the center of early Christianity and the third largest city in the Roman empire, Paul becomes a well-known preacher.

The first journey takes Paul and Barnabas from Antioch to Salamis and Paphos in Cyprus. From there Paul and his companion sail to Perga in Pamphylia and go overland to Pisidian Antioch. From Antioch they travel to Iconium, Lystra, and Derbe before returning by way of the same towns to Antioch, Perga, and Attalia, from where they set sail for Syrian Antioch.

This first journey is the result of a gathering of the Church in Antioch. While the community is in prayer and fasting, they discern that the Holy Spirit wants

Communities and Community in Acts

Paul's First Journey

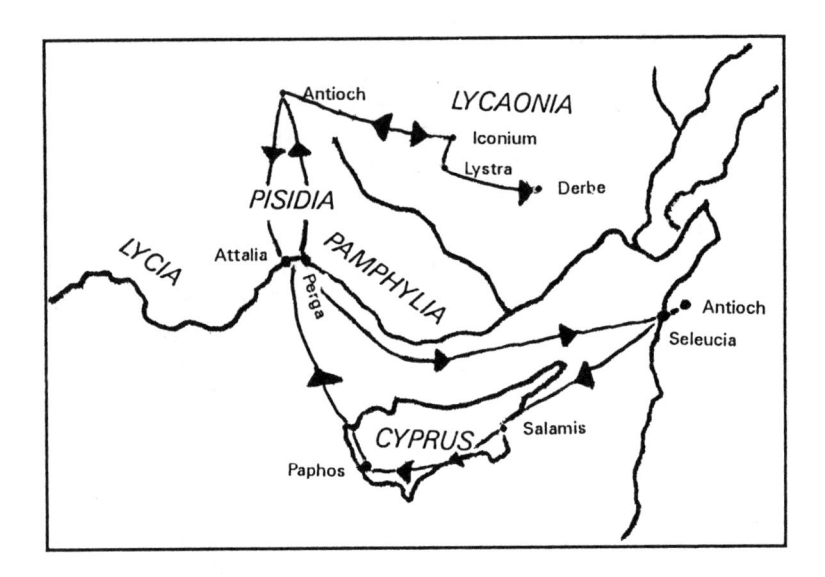

them to set aside Paul and Barnabas for missionary work (Acts 13:2-3). Once chosen, the community lays hands on the two preachers—a practice to which Luke often refers. It is the community that confirms the choice of the Holy Spirit and sets aside some of its members for a special mission. Paul's and Barnabas' practice is to preach in the synagogues and proclaim the Messiahship of Jesus to the Jewish communities.

In Peter's early missionary work, he has a problem with a magician called Simon (Acts 8:9-24); on Paul's first journey, he has a problem with a magician called Elymas (Acts 13:6-12). The story ends with Paul's conversion of the proconsul Sergius Paulus, just as Peter converts the centurion Cornelius. Luke uses parallel incidents in the ministries of Peter and Paul to show that what Peter does in the name of Jesus for the Jews, Paul does in his work for the Gentiles.

Once the disciples arrive in Pisidian Antioch, Paul gives his first major sermon, an inaugural address that summarizes his vision and mission along lines similar to those of Peter's address at Pentecost. The Church at Antioch in Syria saw Paul's mission as the work of the Holy Spirit, and while in Pisidian Antioch, the Holy Spirit leads Paul and Barnabas to a new awareness—that they should go to the Gentiles (Acts 13:46-47). Here, as at other places, persecution leads to expansion of the mission. The missionaries, driven from Antioch, move to Iconium, where they also get a mixed reception. They eventually take refuge in the nearby towns of Lystra and Derbe. In Lystra Paul cures a lame man, just as Peter had done in Jerusalem (Acts 3:1-10). Persecuted in Lystra, the companions move to Derbe and then return through the cities, giving support and encouragement to the new converts and communities they have set up.

This first great journey as described in Acts is a wonderful success, even though Paul makes no mention of it in his letters. Paul and Barnabas establish Christianity in Cyprus, Pisidia, Lycaonia, and Pamphylia. Clearly their interest is not only in individual conversions but more particularly in the founding of churches. One of their great learning experiences is the mission to the Gentiles: "When they arrived [in Antioch], they called the church together and related all that God had done with them, and how he had opened a door of faith for the Gentiles" (Acts 14:27).

Second Missionary Journey

Prior to Paul's and Barnabas' return to Antioch, the apostles held a general council of the Church in Jerusalem to discuss the entrance of Gentiles into the Church. The Christian community in Antioch was divided about Gentile membership as well as the place of Judaism and circumcision in Christian initiation and faith. Some believers held more conservative views, and others more liberal ones.[1] Paul decides to go on a second journey; it is not clear whether he left to encourage the communities he had founded or to get away from the problems and divisiveness of Antioch. He asks Barnabas to go with him, but when the latter wants to take his young cousin Mark, who had abandoned the missionaries on their first journey (Acts 13:13), Paul refuses. The friends quarrel and "the disagreement became so sharp that they parted company" (Acts 15:39). Possibly part of the reason for the parting was that Paul had also criticized Barnabas for joining Peter in refusing to eat with Gentiles (Gal 2:13).

On his second journey, Paul is accompanied by Silas, a leader in the Jerusalem Church who had been sent to Antioch by the apostles with the final report from the Jerusalem Council (Acts 15:22). Paul begins his second journey from Antioch (49-52), traveling north through Syria and then on to Cilicia. He strengthens and consolidates the Christian communities he visits en route (Acts 15:41). He goes on to Derbe and Lystra, cities in which he had established communities during his first journey with Barnabas. While in Lystra, Paul meets a young man named Timothy, who joins Silas and Paul in their missionary work. Although in his letters Paul indicates no knowledge of the decree of the Council of Jerusalem (Acts 15:22-29), Luke insists that as the companions visit one town after another "they delivered to them for observance the decisions that had been reached by the apostles and elders who were in Jerusalem" (Acts 16:4).

Luke returns to the theme that the disciples are constantly guided by the Holy Spirit in their missionary work. The Holy Spirit tells them not to preach neither in Asia nor in Bithynia; in a vision the Spirit directs them to Macedonia, thus leading Paul to Europe and a new stage in his ministry.

Paul's Missionary Journeys

Paul's Second Journey

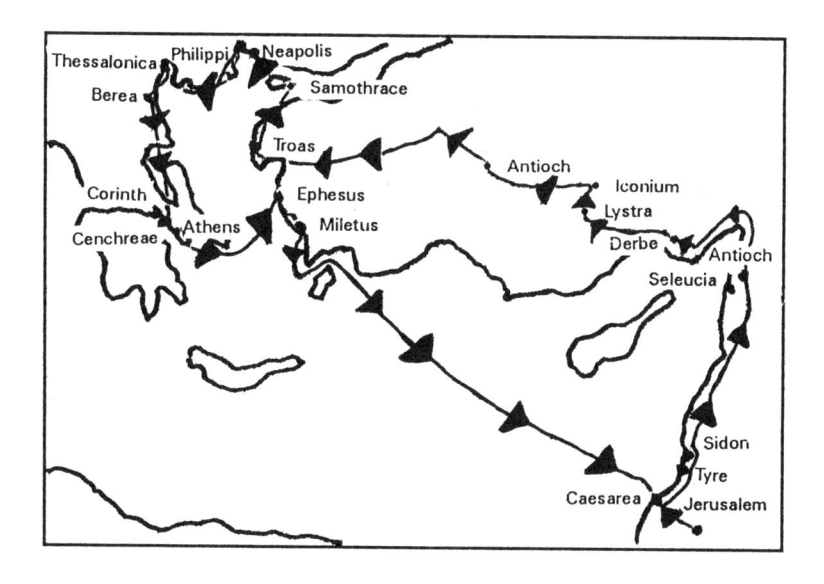

Paul sets out for Europe, and for the first time seems to be accompanied by the writer of Acts, who from this point on refers to the traveling companions as "we." Paul sets sail from Troas, the seaport ten miles south of Troy, and after a break in the journey (probably no more than an overnight stop) on the island of Samothrace, he arrives in northern Greece at the port city of Neapolis. From there he goes inland to Philippi, a Roman colony and the regional capital of Macedonia. Paul and his companions stay several days in Philippi and found a community at Philippi that would become one of Paul's favorites.

After a clash with local figures and resulting flogging and imprisonment, they leave the city to journey on through Amphipolis and Apollonia to Thessalonica, the most important city in Macedonia. Using this city as his base, Paul preaches and again founds a community there (and also a community in the nearby city of

Communities and Community in Acts

Beroea). When some local Jews stir up trouble, the community at Thessalonica decides it is best if Paul leaves. Paul then goes to the coastal area and probably sails to Corinth, leaving behind Silas and Timothy with instructions to join him in Athens.

While in Athens, waiting for his companions to arrive, Paul preaches and teaches, debates with Epicurean and Stoic philosophers, gives his speech before the Areopagus, and makes his first Athenian converts (Acts 17:22-34). Paul, the faithful Jew and zealous Pharisee, must have been appalled by the paganism and excesses he saw in places like Samothrace or Thessalonica. When he arrived in Athens "he was deeply distressed to see that the city was full of idols" (Acts 17:16). Paul never mentions his visit to Athens in his letters, but in Luke's view this city is an important stop on the Gospel's journey to Rome, the center of the world. The Gospel moves from Jerusalem, the religious center, and travels to Athens, the cultural center, before ending in Rome, the political center.

From Athens Paul travels to Corinth, at the time a far more important and larger city than Athens. He arrives there late in the year 50 and stays for about eighteen months—until the spring of 52. He preaches principally, but not exclusively, to the Jews and makes both believers and enemies. The believers establish an important community, and the enemies bring Paul to trial before the proconsul Gallio. (An inscription in Delphi indicates that the proconsul was in Corinth only for about two years, sometime between 51-53; this helps to date Paul's stay in the city.)

Paul stays in Corinth for about eighteen months and with his companions works hard to consolidate the community. While in Corinth, Paul begins to write to former communities to encourage and challenge them in their practice of the faith. Thus, he writes to the Thessalonians around the winter of 51. The reason for his departure from Corinth is not clear, but he leaves from the port of Cenchreae, accompanied by Aquila and Priscilla, and sails to Ephesus. Paul preaches there for a short time, then, leaving behind Aquila and Priscilla, he journeys on to Caesarea, and from there to Antioch.

Third Missionary Journey

Paul leaves Corinth at the end of his second journey, around the spring of 52, passing through Ephesus and Caesarea before returning to Antioch, the city from which he departed in 49. However, it seems he was back in Ephesus by the end of 52, so there must not have been a break between the end of the second journey and the beginning of the third. Acts tells us that he travels through Galatia and Phrygia (Acts 18:23), but does not mention whether he passes through his hometown of Tarsus. Ephesus was his base of operations for his second journey, and he stays there about two and a half years. Paul preaches first in the synagogue for about three months (Acts 19:8). Later, after a conflict with the Jews, he spends two years holding daily discussions in the lecture room of Tyrannus (Acts 19:9).

Paul's ministry in Ephesus is very successful, and people from all over the region come to listen to him (Acts 19:10,17,20). It is possible that while in Ephesus he writes the first and parts of the second letters to the Corinthians. He makes plans to journey through Macedonia and Achaia and sends co-workers ahead of him to prepare the way (Acts 19:21-22). When Paul sets out, he travels by way of the cities he had visited on his second journey. "When he had gone through those regions and had given the believers much encouragement, he came to Greece, where he stayed for three months" (Acts 20:2-3).

It seems Paul planned to leave the province of Achaia (probably Corinth) by sea just as he did on his first visit

Paul's Third Journey

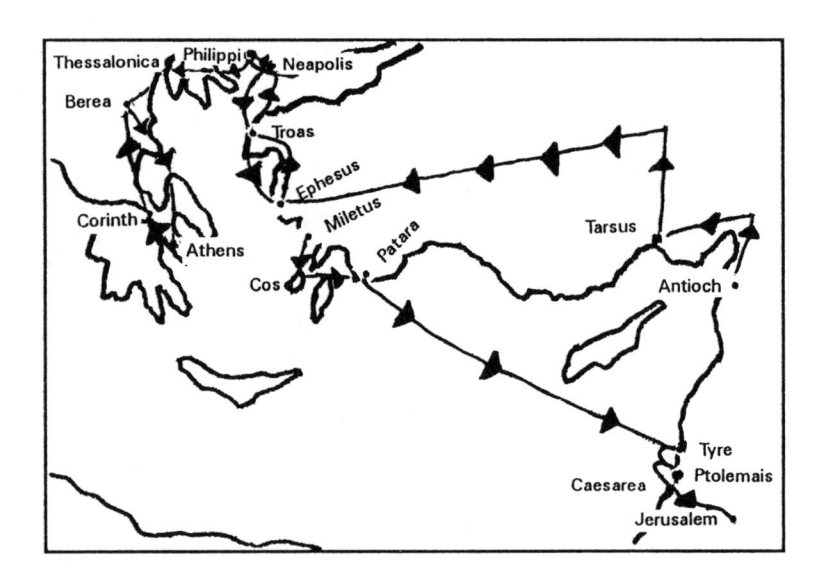

there. The Jews organize a plot against Paul, and he decides to thwart their efforts by changing his plans and returning through Macedonia, sailing from Philippi to Troas, where he meets up with co-workers who have traveled directly from Achaia. Paul stays in Troas for a week, preaching and celebrating the Breaking of Bread with the local community. Leaving the community, Paul's companions sail along the coast, stopping at Assos to pick up Paul, who had decided to travel overland. From there they all sail south, stopping at several towns until they reach Miletus. Paul sends for the elders of the Church at Ephesus, and Luke presents Paul's third great discourse in Acts.

Leaving the Ephesian elders, the companions sail to Cos, Rhodes, and Patara. From there they sail around the south side of Cyprus and arrive at Tyre, where they spend a week with the local community. From Tyre the missionaries travel to Ptolemais, staying a day with the local community, then on to Caesarea, where they stay with Philip, one of the original seven deacons. Here as in Tyre and elsewhere, believers urge Paul not to go to Jerusalem. In fact, Paul acknowledges to the Ephesian elders, "And now, as a captive to the Spirit, I am on my way to Jerusalem, not knowing what will happen to me there, except that the Holy Spirit testifies to me in every city that imprisonment and persecutions are waiting for me" (Acts 20:22-23). Nevertheless, Paul and his co-workers set out from Caesarea for Jerusalem, where he receives a warm welcome from the leaders, a cautious response from some believers, and persecution from the Jews. Thus ends Paul's third journey.

Paul's Final Journey in Acts

In the Third Gospel, Luke tells us three times about the passion that awaits Jesus. Likewise in Acts, Luke tells us three times about the passion that awaits Paul. Jesus' journey ended in Jerusalem, and Paul's begins there and ends in Rome. Paul's journey is that of the model minister who imitates the Lord.

Although Paul tries to oblige the leaders of the Jerusalem Church, who want him to present himself as observant of the Law (Acts 21:20-24), their efforts do not succeed. Some Jews, recognizing Paul in the Temple, seize him and drag him to kill him. As often happens in Acts, the Romans intervene to protect Church figures.[2] In this incident, the tribune decides to take Paul to the Fortress Antonia.

Paul stops and gives a speech in which he recounts his original conversion. When he speaks about his mission to the Gentiles, the Jews begin to riot. Once in the fortress, the tribune instructs the soldiers to flog Paul as a way of forcing him to confess the crime he committed that so infuriated the crowds.

Hearing that Paul is a Roman citizen, the tribune frees him and calls for a meeting of the Sanhedrin to

Communities and Community in Acts

Paul's Fourth Journey

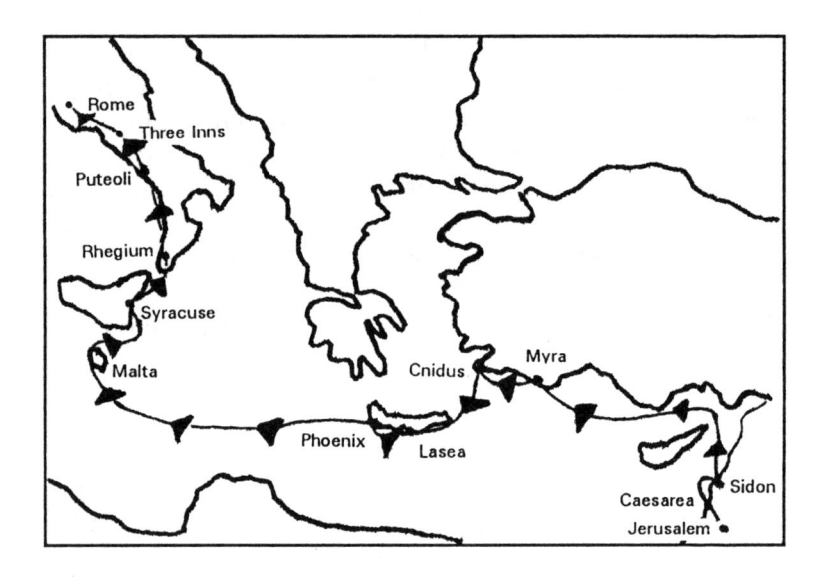

determine Paul's guilt—as in the Gospel when they gathered to determine Jesus' guilt. At the meeting Paul skillfully sets the Pharisees against the Sadducees, a tactic that almost leads to another riot and forces the intervention of the tribune.

After learning of a plot to kill Paul, the tribune arranges for an armed escort to take him to the Roman governor, Felix, who arranges for the case to be heard in Caesarea. Felix, like other procurators, is known for his corruption and keeps Paul under house arrest for two years, hoping to get money from him (Acts 24:26). In 58 Felix is replaced by Festus. Festus reopens Paul's case, but Paul, seeing that Festus wants to ingratiate himself to the Jews at his expense, uses his Roman privilege and appeals to Caesar. Festus invites King Agrippa to attend a later meeting with Paul; as happened with Felix, the local Roman authorities declare Paul innocent (Acts 25:27; 26:32).

Paul is entrusted to the Roman centurion Julius of the Augustan cohort; he is accompanied by Aristarchus and, some writers suggest, the author of Acts (Acts 27:1). They sail north along the coast to Sidon, where the centurion allows Paul to visit members of the local community (Acts 27:3). Due to strong headwinds, they sail from Sidon around the northeast corner of Cyprus. They take two weeks to arrive at the port of Myra in Lycia. From here Paul's journey should have taken him north past Rhodes to Cnidus, but strong winds again force the ship to turn south and seek shelter along the southern shore of Crete. They eventually rest in Fair Havens, just west of Lasea, in late September or early October. Paul warns the centurion and other travelers of danger ahead, but they ignore him, deciding instead to sail further along the coast and winter in the port town of Phoenix.

However, a great wind blows up from the northeast and drives the ship out to the open sea, past the island of Cauda into the open Mediterranean. By some estimates, 276 people are on board, and they do all they can to save the ship, jettisoning the cargo, tackle, and even food. Paul encourages everyone to brave the storm. He assures them of survival, guides the soldiers, and advises the centurion. After drifting for fourteen nights, the group eventually lands on the island of Malta. In telling this story of Paul's shipwreck, Luke no doubt wants to tell us about God's guidance and protection of this missionary and explain how, through visions and miracles, Paul's greatness is appreciated by non-believers.

They stay in Malta for three months, a time for Paul to preach and heal. From Malta they sail on an Alexandrian ship to Syracuse. The ship passes on the eastern side of Sicily to Rhegium and then to Puteoli, where Paul meets members of the local Christian community. From there they travel north, overland to Rome. Paul meets believers who wait for his arrival at the

Forum of Appius and the Three Taverns. When Paul reaches Rome, he arrives at the center of the known world. Christian communities there are already flourishing, but with his arrival Paul fulfills Jesus' commission and Luke achieves one of his great aims—to bring the Gospel to the ends of the earth.

A Sense of Community in the Early Church

Coming Together in Faith

After the death of Jesus and some initial hesitancy on the part of the disciples, Luke tells us that they gather in the upper room to await the coming of the Holy Spirit according to the Lord's directions. What brings them together is belief in the Lord's resurrection (Acts 2:24,32; 4:2,10), a desire for a new life in Christ (Acts 2:40; 4:12), and a readiness to repent (Acts 3:19) and be baptized (Acts 2:38). They strongly believe that the gathering of the Church is God's work among them, "and day by day the Lord added to their number those who were being saved" (Acts 2:47). Conscious of the Lord's continuous guidance, the disciples quickly become active in missionary work, preaching and healing in the name of the Lord Jesus. Luke portrays the remarkable growth of the Church; he is convinced that this growth is part of the plan of God—a plan that includes peace and the comfort of the Holy Spirit (Acts 9:31).

Luke portrays the Father guiding the Church by sending the Holy Spirit (Acts 1:4-5; 5:32), by confirming ministers' work through the power of miracles (Acts 2:43; 5:12-14; 15:12; 19:11), by giving directions through visions (10:1-23; 16:9), and by sending angels to carry out the divine plan (Acts 8:26; 12:7). Believers see themselves as God's people. They pray to God (Acts 4:24-30; 21:20) and recognize that the Church's success comes from God (Acts 19:20; 21:19).

The community of believers share a common vision: salvation can only be found in Jesus (Acts 4:12; 22:16). Thus they call upon his name (Acts 2:21), accept baptism in his name (Acts 2:38; 8:16; 10:48; 19:5), work miracles in his name (Acts 3:6; 16; 4:10,30; 16:18), and teach in his name (Acts 4:18; 5:28). They also suffer for his name (Acts 5:41; 9:16; 21:13), preach the power of the name (Acts 8:12; 9:15,28), proclaim forgiveness of sin in his name (Acts 10:43), and pray in the name of the Lord Jesus (Acts 9:14,21; 19:17).

Called by the Father and founded on the name of Jesus, this community is the result of the gift of the Holy Spirit, poured out upon believers at the foundation of their communities (Acts 2:1-4; 8:14-17; 10:44; 19:6). The Holy Spirit gives authority to the Church (Acts 20:28) and guides it (Acts 16:7; 20:23). Luke sees the Holy Spirit so identified with the Church that they testify as one (Acts 5:29-32). Betrayal of the Church is betrayal of the Holy Spirit, as Ananias and Sapphira discover (Acts 5:3).

Christian communities in Acts see themselves as special people, called by God, dedicated to Jesus, and guided by the Holy Spirit. They are aware of themselves as a special group, and other people hold them in high respect (Acts 5:13). They gather in the Temple and in each other's homes (Acts 5:42) and develop a community life of intense sharing (Acts 2:42-47; 4:32-35). Gradually they extend themselves to the Gentiles and bring both the Word and their communal life to the cultural and political centers of the world.

Membership in the Community

One of the pervading elements in Acts is the relationship of Christianity to Judaism. Luke's geographical

Communities and Community in Acts

plan—a movement from Jerusalem to Judea, Samaria, the sea coast, and the Gentile world of Athens and Rome—is also his theological departure from Judaism, testifying to his conviction that the Church needs to accept its own identity, an identity distinct from Judaism and dedicated to the Gentile world. The transition from a Jewish-centered faith is not easily achieved. Once missionaries recognize this problem (Acts 15:1-3), the apostles gather to discuss and resolve it (Acts 15:6-29). However, difficulties remain throughout the missionary work of Acts. Paul's final words are both an historical and theological turning point for the Church (Acts 28:28).

The development of the Church's missions shows the great success of the Gospel. The believers hold an exclusive view of their faith—they do not merge with other religions. They require a total and exclusive commitment to the Lord in the Church (Acts 9:4). Their resulting faith is permeated with hope—hope in salvation, final conquest of evil, and the return of the Lord in glory.

Peter lists the basic conditions for membership as repentance, belief in Jesus, baptism and reception of the Holy Spirit (Acts 2:38). Nevertheless, membership is essentially a gift from the Lord, who blesses whomever he wishes with "the repentance that leads to life" (Acts 11:18). The members strengthen their community life with personal and communal prayer in each other's home and with the ritual celebration of the Breaking of Bread. "They devoted themselves to the apostles' teaching and fellowship, the breaking of bread and the prayers" (Acts 2:42). They share their material possessions with each other and insure that there are no needy people in their midst (Acts 4:32-35). They constantly support each other in the profession of faith; for example, Paul and Barnabas travel back to the cities in which they founded churches to encourage believers to persevere in their commitment.

In Acts, membership in the community of faith implies an active commitment. Many believers, frequently under the inspiration of the Holy Spirit, leave their communities to go on mission, as did Paul and Barnabas, Timothy, Silas, and Mark. Apollo and the married couple, Aquila and his wife Priscilla, respond to the evangelizing needs of the Church.

The community maintains fidelity to its vision and life by obedience to the Word and Spirit. Luke sometimes identifies the Word with the community (Acts 12:24; 19:20), and sometimes he identifies the Spirit with the community (Acts 5:3). As they live together they constantly discern the will of God. The community must be obedient to the Word for it forms and guides them, but the Word has a power of its own, spreading and growing and making converts (Acts 6:7; 12:24). Luke tells us the disciples "praised the word of the Lord" (Acts 13:48).

The Holy Spirit guides the community through Scripture (Acts 4:25), Church leaders (Acts 15:28), local prophets (Acts 11:28-30; 21:10-11), and entire communities (Acts 21:4-6). On occasions the Spirit guides the community to action (Acts 5:32), sometimes to inaction (Acts 16:6). Obedience to this inspiration is required of all believers, whether individuals (Acts 10:44-48) or communities (Acts 13:1-3).

Community in Acts and Community Today

According to Acts, the apostolic figures of early Christianity, men and women alike, energetically and enthusiastically spread the Word and share their newfound faith with everyone throughout the known world of their time. With so little, materially and educationally, they travel so far and do so much. Although they face struggles at every turn, they evidence boldness and constant joy in their work of evangelization. Faithful to the call of the Lord, they are convinced that the Word is for everyone to receive not passively, but to receive and hand on. As they form communities, the believers become evangelizing communities. The early Church gradually becomes a universal community made up of smaller communities. The great conviction that the missionary vocation is for every baptized believer helps to foster a sense of responsibility for the faith.

As we look at our ecclesial communities today, we can be enthused by Luke and his challenge to spread the faith. His apostolic heroes never become complacent. Despite trials, they bring the Word to new situations. When some welcome the message they rejoice, and when others reject it they accept the pain and re-present the message. Whatever believers do in Acts, the Word always retains primacy. Proclaiming the Word is, and always must be, the irresistible challenge in the life of every believer.

For Personal and Group Reflection

1. The zeal of the early missionaries contributes powerfully to the spread of the Gospel. Is this same zeal found in individuals and parishes today? Exemplify.

2. The New Testament Church faces many problems—both internal divisiveness and external persecution. Do local churches struggle through their problems without bitterness and polarization?

3. The Holy Spirit guides the missionary expansion of the early Church. Are you, as a dedicated Christian and minister, always open in prayer and reflection to the guidance of the Holy Spirit in your life and ministry?

4. Acts frequently shows links between the acceptance of suffering and the spread of the Gospel; suffering and death lead to new life for the Church as they did for Jesus. In our modern culture, which tries to avoid suffering, how do you and your community integrate suffering into your Christian commitment and ministry?

5. In Acts, communities choose their leaders, who then receive the Church's mandate through the imposition of hands by the apostles. How can communities today be involved in the choice of their ministers?

6. In Acts, each community sets aside some of its members for evangelization, sending them as missionaries to other regions. How can modern parishes fulfill their missionary responsibilities?

7. In Acts, the Church preaches the Word of God in the major religious, cultural, and political centers of the Mediterranean world. Paul especially has a preference for large metropolitan areas in spite of all their complicated social and moral problems. Do you treat Christianity in the same way, as a major influence in religious, cultural, political, and moral life?

8. Acts portrays individuals, married couples, and significant women in key missionary, evangelizing, educational, and leadership roles. Is leadership in ministry too restrictive in your church? What roles do laity, single men and women, and married couples have?

9. Luke identifies the essential components of community life for the early Church

(see pages 54-58). Are these reflected in your contemporary communities, families, and friendships?

10. The Church in Acts reaches out to the outcasts of its own day—the Samaritans and Gentiles. Who are the outcasts of our own times to whom our Church needs to reach out?

Chapter Three

Luke's Purpose in Writing Acts

> I...decided, after investigating everything carefully from the very first, to write an orderly account for you, most excellent Theophilus, so that you may know the truth concerning the things about which you have been instructed (Lk 1:3-4).

Mark wrote the first Gospel around 65-70, a challenging but short synthesis of Jesus' teachings. Later Matthew, Luke, and John wrote Gospels for their communities, each one giving different emphases. Mark's Gospel has sixteen chapters, Matthew has twenty-eight chapters, and John has twenty-one chapters. Luke writes a total of fifty-two chapters in his Gospel and Acts combined—more than any other New Testament writer.

Why did Luke write a new Gospel? This is an important question, but an even more important questions is: Why write Acts, a type of work that no one else wrote for the Church? Further, what did Luke hope to achieve by writing these two volumes? Which specific needs in the Church did he think this work would address? In

Luke's Purpose in Writing Acts

his retelling of the story of Jesus in his Gospel, he identifies themes and concerns that Mark never addresses, and in Acts he focuses on the Church. In Acts he presents a vision that has influenced every successive generation of believers.

Luke is a great storyteller who writes in an elegant Greek that would have attracted the intelligentsia of his day. He also has a great love for people and gives us attractive portraits of more exemplary individuals than any other New Testament writer. Luke is one of the great theologians of the early Church, but he does not give us abstract statements or systematic, theoretical theology. Rather, he seems more like a pastor and spiritual guide, and in his writings "we are witnessing the beginnings of pastoral theology" (O'Neill, "Six Amen Sayings," 9). He not only repeats the authentic message of Jesus and the early Church but conveys a sense of responsibility for it, proclaiming it with freshness for his own community and future ones, too. He gives us the essentials of the history of the early Church, and he is a literary and theological artist who reframes the Church's teachings in ways people of every generation can find clear, relevant, and challenging, and to which they can respond with enthusiasm, hope, and love.

In searching for the purpose of Acts, we will have to consider Luke-Acts together, since Luke wrote them as a unit and because the plan, themes, and theology of one permeate the other. In fact, it is legitimate to ask: "Is the unified work of a different genre than either taken individually?" (Juel 2-3). Writers, ancient or modern, do not generally write for one reason alone. They often write for several reasons—some primary and others secondary. In looking at Acts we will examine Luke's aims by considering his major compositional features, those aspects of the work that evidence his specific editorial contributions. We will look at the recurring themes he finds in the tradition and in his sources, since his repetition of these themes indicates their importance. We will review some of the new emphases Luke introduces in his work, new theological directions that he as a pastoral leader suggests. Finally we will summarize the theological focuses that permeate Luke's writing of Acts.

Major Compositional Features in Acts

Literary Techniques in Acts

Every writer has his or her own way of communicating ideas. Sometimes a person's style and skills are appreciated by others and sometimes not. Mark, one of Luke's sources, in places has an inelegant and clumsy style; thus the other two Synoptic writers do not imitate Mark's literary technique but use their own. Sometimes a writer presents a theological position that others find unpersuasive, as Luke and Matthew do regarding Mark's messianic secret.[1]

Luke is an outstanding writer, the educated and cultured figure of New Testament times; he has the most extensive Greek vocabulary of any New Testament writer. He writes in a polished style, as can be seen in the substantial editing he does of Mark's rough and clumsy presentations. He demonstrates openness and flexibility in adapting his material to his own audience. He clarifies obscure ideas in his sources and modifies a Jewish-based tradition for his Gentile audience.

Luke's literary techniques not only serve the style of his presentation, but several of them significantly aid his pastoral goals. He uses the Jewish Scriptures extensively, weaving its teachings throughout his work in such a way that any Jews in his audience would appreciate the links. He does this in an unobtrusive way so that these Scriptures never prove difficult for the Gentiles (who make up the largest portion of his audience). Luke is also aware of the religious and secular interests of the Hellenistic world and so integrates these themes and literary formats to arouse interest and excitement among Hellenistic readers.

Luke uses literary techniques to create an atmosphere conducive to the reception of the message he presents. He composes summary statements that give general descriptions of the life of the early Church (Acts 2:43-47; 4:32-37; 5:12-16; 9:31). Written in the imperfect tense in Greek, these summaries do not chronicle specific events but give a general picture of the kind of life to which believers dedicate themselves. Moreover, these summaries are helpful in appreciating values that consistently motivate the early Church.

Luke punctuates the narrative of Acts with short statements that serve like a chorus in a song. These refrains repeat Lukan motifs and create the atmosphere in which the message should be received. He often pauses to speak of believers' joy (Acts 8:8,39; 13:48,52; 16:34) or of the successful expansion and growth of the early Church (Acts 2:41; 28:31).

We have seen that Luke likes to balance his narratives by paralleling episodes in Acts with episodes in his Gospel (Lk 4:14-30 and Acts 2:1-36; Lk 23:34-36 and Acts 7:59-60; Lk 7:11-17 and Acts 9:33-35; Lk 8:40-42,49-56 and Acts 9:36-43). Episodes in the second part of Acts, which deals with Paul, balance episodes in the first half, which deals with Peter (Acts 2:14-41 and 13:16-41; 8:9-24 and 13:6-11; 3:1-10 and 14:8-10; 5:15-16 and 19:11-12). This technique not only creates harmony in the work but shows how God confirms Paul's ministry with the same signs as Peter's (Acts 3:2-10 and 14:8-10; 5:15 and 19:12; 5:16 and 16:18; 8:18-24 and 13:6-12; 9:36-43 and 20:9-10).[2] Furthermore, the paralleling manifests Luke's conviction concerning the harmony that exists, or should exist, between the Jewish and Gentile worlds, both of which are blessed with the same grace of God. Another part of Luke's balancing technique is his use of stories about men and stories about women, thereby showing their equality before God. Luke gives us Zechariah and Elizabeth, Mary and Joseph, Simeon and Anna, the man who loses a sheep and the woman who loses a coin, the raising of the servant of the centurion and the raising of the son of the widow of Nain, the Twelve and the women who accompany Jesus.

Luke avoids needless repetition, and when he finds it in his sources he omits it. However, on two occasions in Acts he repeats a story three times in order to give it great emphasis. Both instances relate important aspects of his vision of Church. The first story tells of the conversion of the first Gentile, Cornelius (Acts 10:9-16,23-48; 11:1-18), and the second tells of the call of Paul, the Apostle of the Gentiles (Acts 9:1-18; 22:6-16; 26:12-18).

Gentile Conventions

The overwhelming opinion among commentators is that Luke was a Gentile writing for a predominantly Gentile audience. Acts contains a preface, letters, speeches, journey narratives, and a sea voyage—features common to Greco-Roman writing. His knowledge of both classical and *koiné* Greek, his sentence structure, and his reference to a patron in the preface indicate either his own background, his audience's background, or both.

The Emmaus story, in which Jesus joins the travelers (Lk 24:13-35), and Philip's apparition before the Ethiopian minister (Acts 8:26-40) reflect the classical theme of the "divine tramp." Likewise the episode in which the people place their sick on the street in order that Peter's shadow will fall over them is similar to a story from

Greek literature that describes the miraculous activity of the philosopher, Apollonius of Tyana (Acts 5:15). When Luke describes the life of the early Church, he makes implicit reference to the ideal picture of Plato's *Republic* (Acts 4:34). Luke presents Paul's dialogues with the Stoics and Epicureans in his visit to Athens (Acts 17:22-31), and Luke's presentation of the sea voyage in Paul's last journey parallels the typical sea voyages of Greek literature (Acts 27:1-28:15). These examples suggest Luke's desire to be considered an intelligent participant in the literary life of the Mediterranean world.

The speeches in Acts are a further example of a Gentile literary practice. They amount to nearly three quarters of the book and are given principally by Peter and Paul. Paul's speeches do not correspond with the vocabulary and theology we find in his letters. Peter's do not correspond with the two letters attributed to him or with the ideas in Mark, were the latter to be viewed, as tradition suggests, as the work of a secretary to Peter. The speeches are not totally free, creative writings originating from sources distinct from Luke's other work, which might imply they were the work of Paul or Peter; rather, they are well inserted into the context of Luke's narrative. They each contain similar themes and follow a similar format, thus leading to the conclusion that the speech writer is indeed Luke. Luke uses these speeches to summarize the Gospel.[3] These Lukan compositions follow the same outline, reflect themes common in the early Church's evangelization,[4] and contain distinctive Lukan theology.[5] Moreover, by being organized in the same way and emphasizing the same themes, the speeches are a fine aid in learning the Gospel message. Many writers and commentators recognize that this common format of Luke's is a useful technique for memorizing and catechizing. For preachers in the Hellenistic world, these speeches were similarly useful. Some commentators believe that the speeches are in the form of Greco-Roman legal briefs; in Acts Luke uses them as supportive presentations to persuade Theophilus about the legitimacy of Christianity and the innocence of Paul.

The central section of Luke's Gospel is a journey narrative (Lk 9:51-19:27); in fact the Third Gospel frequently uses journeys. As we saw in the last chapter, Acts also develops by means of journeys. In Greek literature one can find the theme of journey in the *Iliad* and the *Odyssey*, and Luke, ever sensitive to the interests of his audience, develops the narrative of his great heroes through journeys.[6] For Paul's final journey, Luke uses "what could be called a characteristically Gentile story," a sea voyage that has parallels with sea journey stories in ancient literature" (Praeder 704).

The Structure of Acts

Acts and the Third Gospel go together and share a similar structure, and some subsections parallel each other. Both have a preface, a period of religious renewal in readiness for baptism, a baptismal experience, several periods of ministry, and a final journey, which is a period of ministry that also reveals important theological insights. Jesus' journey reveals who Christ is, and Paul's journey reveals the nature of discipleship.

When looking at Acts as a whole, some commentators (like Kümmel) simply divide it into two large sections corresponding to a Petrine section (chapters 1-12) and a Pauline section (chapters 13-28). The two sections deal respectively with the Gospel's move from Jerusalem to Antioch and from Antioch to Rome. Another way of looking at Acts as a simple two-fold division is to view it as the securing of the Gentile mission (chapters 1-15) and the expansion of that mission to Rome (chapters 15-28).

Luke's Purpose in Writing Acts

Some commentators point out that Luke writes in blocks and often summarizes his material at the end of a section. They point to noticeable breaks in the narrative, highlighted by summary statements or refrains (Acts 6:7; 9:31; 11:18; 12:24; 14:28; 16:5; 19:5). Such breaks help illustrate the division of Acts.

1:1-5	Preface
1:6-4:22	Period of Preparation for the Ministry of the Church

Ministries of the Church

4:23-8:3	Ministry in Jerusalem
8:4-11:18	Ministry in Samaria
11:19-15:35	Ministry in the Antiochean region
15:36-21:3	Ministry around the Aegean Sea
21:4-28:31	A Ministry Journey to Rome

We have already seen that Luke wishes to show in Acts how the Church is faithful to Jesus' final commission (Lk 24:47-48; Acts 1:8). Acts unfolds in a way that gradually describes the Church's expansion of ministry from Jerusalem, through Judea and Samaria to the coastal region and then on to Rome, the center of the empire.

Detailed Outline of Acts of Apostles

1:1-5	Preface: The work is dedicated to Theophilus and deals with what is done through the Holy Spirit by the chosen apostles of Jesus.

Preparation for the Ministry of the Church

1:6-14	The gathering of Spirit-filled witnesses to the initiative of God. The Church to

Major Compositional Features in Acts

	be born will be filled with the Holy Spirit.
1:15-26	The Church will be the new Israel.
2:1-36	Birth of the Church, a community for all nations.
2:37-41	Preparations for the coming ministry of the Lord—a sermon.
1:14	The disciples pray as they await their baptism.
2:1-4	The Spirit fills the disciples.
2:5-13	Implication of the universality of the Church's ministry.
2:42-47	Clarification of the nature of ministry—to "be Church."
3:1-4:22	The Church's ministry begins with a sermon, but the Sanhedrin arrests the apostles.

Ministries of the Church

Each period in the Church's ministry presents similar characteristics. There is always the description of a call to ministry and an endowment of the power of the God's Spirit. The minister presents a Christ-centered proclamation which is always rejected by some of the audience. Although persecution inevitably follows, the Church ministry continues to progress.

4:23-8:3	Ministry in Jerusalem
4:23-6:4	Peter and the Twelve
6:5-8:3	Stephen
8:4-11:18	Ministry in Samaria
8:4-40	Philip in Samaria and Gaza

Luke's Purpose in Writing Acts

    9:1-31   Saul
    9:32-11:18   Peter in Lydda, Joppa and Caesarea
11:19-15:35   Ministry in the Antiochean region
      11:19-30   The Church's ministry in Antioch
      13:1-15:35   Barnabas and Saul on a first great journey
15:36-21:3   Ministry around the Aegean Sea
      16:1-17:15   Paul and Silas as far as Europe
      17:16-18:28   Paul in Athens and Corinth
      19:1-21:3   Paul in Ephesus and back to Caesarea

21:4-28:30: The Minister's Dedication, Even to Death

A Journey Ministry to Rome

    21:4-5   Prayer
    21:5-12   Awareness of what lies ahead
    21:13-14   Paul's recommitment and self-gift
    21:17-26:32   Temptations—people unclear about the nature of Paul's ministry
      21:17-40   Rejected by his own Church
      22:1-29   Rejected by the Jewish crowds
      22:30-23:11   Rejected by the Jewish leaders
      23:23-25:12   The state uninterested in the issue
      25:13-26:32   Rejected by other political leaders
    27:1-28:22   A journey to death
    28:23-28   Ministry ends in rejection
    28:30   The Church's ministry continues

Recurring Themes in Acts

Church's Mission of Salvation

Hans Conzelmann, the great German scholar who is justly credited with beginning a new era of Lukan studies, proposes that Luke's primary interest is salvation history. Conzelmann—whose commentary on the Gospel of Luke is titled *The Theology of St. Luke*—believes Luke's primary concern is to calm the anxiety of those Christians who, having expected the immediate return of the Lord, find their hopes unmet. According to Conzelmann, Luke presents his work in three phases corresponding to three stages in the historical unfolding of salvation: a period of promise, seen in the Jewish Scriptures and in Luke's infancy narratives, a period of fulfillment, seen in Jesus' ministry in the Gospel, and a period when the message is extended to the ends of the earth, as seen in Acts. These three periods, of which Jesus' ministry is "the middle time," are each part of the great plan of God. Luke suggests believers should not be disturbed by the delay of the second coming for, he insists, the delay is part of God's plan. Thus, according to Conzelmann and others, Luke is the theologian of salvation history. His work is a pastoral response to believers' concerns, assuring them of the importance of this "third period" and the importance of their contributions to the development of the Church.

I. Howard Marshall has frequently taken issue with Conzelmann and claims that Luke does not focus on salvation history but rather on the nature of salvation offered in Jesus. For Marshall, salvation is presented in the Gospel, where we meet "the Son of Man [who] came to seek out and to save the lost" (Lk 19:10). The purpose of Acts, then, is to show the spread of this Word of salvation. To those who seek salvation the early preachers can say: "Believe on the Lord Jesus, and

Luke's Purpose in Writing Acts

you will be saved" (Acts 16:31). While Acts has a variety of motifs and secondary themes, the principal purpose is to present the Lord's message of salvation, for salvation is through Christ and his Word. In the beginning of the Gospel (in the infancy narrative), Jesus is recognized as the savior (Lk 2:11); by the end of Acts the news that he is savior is proclaimed to the ends of the earth. Only in his name can the world receive salvation (Acts 4:12; 10:43; 22:16). In Marshall's view, Acts is the story of the growth of the Church because it is the story of the spread of salvation. For Marshall, Luke is not concerned with the history of salvation but with the nature of salvation: Luke's primary aim is not to present history but to evangelize.[7]

Other writers emphasize Luke's interest in salvation but are convinced he focuses his presentation not on the history of salvation or the theology of salvation but on the pastoral concern of making that salvation universal through the welcoming of Gentiles into the Church. On the only two occasions Luke repeats a story, he does so to emphasize the salvation of the Gentiles: the conversion of Paul, Apostle of the Gentiles, and the conversion of Cornelius, the first Gentile welcomed into the Church. In Acts God declares Paul "an instrument whom I have chosen to bring my name before Gentiles" (9:15). After Cornelius' conversion, the Church praises God, saying, "Then God has given even to the Gentiles the repentance that leads to life" (Acts 11:18).

During Paul's first missionary journey, he gives a sermon in Pisidian Antioch. After some negative reaction from Jews in the city, he and Barnabas declare that they will direct their ministry to the Gentiles (Acts 13:46-48). Returning to Antioch from their first journey, "they called the Church together and related all that God had done with them, and how he had opened a door of faith for the Gentiles" (Acts 14:27). During the Council of Jerusalem, Paul and Barnabas report on the conversion of the Gentiles, to the delight of the Church (Acts 15:3,12); in fact, the apostles decide to adapt their pastoral practice to respond to the needs of Gentiles (Acts 15:23-29). While in Corinth during his second journey, Paul again clashes with the local Jews and tells them, "From now on I will go to the Gentiles" (Acts 18:6). At the end of his third journey Paul goes to Jerusalem and relates all the great things God has done among the Gentiles through his ministry (Acts 21:19). Luke's second volume ends with Paul declaring to the Jews in Rome, "Let it be known to you then that this salvation of God has been sent to the Gentiles; they will listen" (28:28).

Luke's second volume provides us with the gradual and successful expansion of the Gospel to the Gentile world. We have already seen how he does this in stages, describing the conversions of Samaritans, a Jewish proselyte, a devout Gentile, and then Gentiles in general. Luke also emphasizes the Church's mission to the Gentiles at key places in the structure of Luke-Acts: at the beginning of the ministry in the Gospel (Lk 3:6) and at the conclusion of Acts (28:28); at the end of the first volume (Lk 24:47) and at the beginning of the second (Acts 1:8). Moreover, the inaugural speeches of Luke's key heroes—Jesus (Lk 4:16-30), Peter (Acts 2:14-40), and Paul (Acts 13:15-52)—all refer to the Gentile mission. Again, the only time he repeats stories is to stress the importance of the Gentile entry into the Church.[8]

The issues of salvation are crucial to Luke's presentation of the message. The various opinions of scholars do not need to be mutually exclusive. Luke shows us how God unfolds the divine plan for salvation, clarifies its nature, and challenges us to be aware of this plan that it is available to everyone.

The Church's Relationship with the Empire

Some writers consider Luke-Acts to be a description of the Christian community in dialogue with the State. Others see the two volumes as a defense of the religion before the Roman authorities. More recently, commentators have suggested that Luke is defending the empire before the Church.

Luke writes both volumes to Theophilus, who is possibly a Roman official, since Luke gives him the title "most excellent" (Lk 1:3; Acts 1:1). The evangelist says he is writing to the official "so that you may know the truth concerning the things about which you have been instructed" (Lk 1:4). The word "instructed" would probably be better translated as "informed"; many commentators think Luke is writing to explain in more detail the truth concerning the things of which Theophilus has been informed, presumably by Christianity's enemies.

When Rome conquered a nation, it commonly destroyed the religions of that nation, save one; the remaining religion was meant to unify the conquered people. Thus in Palestine after the end of the war in 70 CE, only Judaism was left as the national religion. It was the only permissible religion, the *religio licita*. For the Roman rulers, who were for the most part uninterested in the religious practices of Palestine, Judaism was a religion divided into various sects: Pharisees, Sadducees, Essenes, and Zealots. In the years just after the death of Jesus, these leaders saw Christians as yet another sect of Judaism for three reasons: Christian and Jewish beliefs were similar, Christians considered themselves to be the outgrowth of Judaism, and they met in the Temple. However, around the year 83 CE, local Jewish leaders excommunicated Christians from the synagogues, and by 90 CE the Jewish leaders of Jamnia had formally broken with the followers of Jesus, declaring them to be heretics. This was not only a signal to Jews but also to the Romans that this group was no longer part of the official *religio licita*. In this historical context Luke writes to Theophilus. A. R. C. Leaney states it this way: "There can be little doubt that Luke was influenced, among other considerations, by the desirability of showing that Christianity was politically innocent" (5), and G. B. Caird refers to Luke's work as "the first great apologia for the Christian faith" (14).

Authors who support this view point to Luke's constant interest in presenting to Rome a favorable picture of Christianity. John the Baptist preaches to the Roman soldiers, who are receptive to his message (Lk 3:14). Jesus heals a centurion's slave (Lk 7:1-10) and taught the legitimacy of paying taxes to the emperor (Lk 20:21-26). Pilate, Rome's regional governor, declares Jesus innocent (Lk 23:13-16), as does the centurion at the foot of the cross (Lk 23:47). Thus, Luke insists that Christ and implicitly his followers "have justly been pronounced innocent by the representatives of Roman law" (Caird 14). Moreover, when Luke describes the Jews in Acts, he "describes them as notorious disturbers of the peace" (Conzelmann 145). He consistently proposes that Christianity can have a positive effect on the social and moral standards of the empire.[9]

Some writers take a different view of Luke's apologetic approach, suggesting that it is not Christianity that he is defending but Paul. According to this view, Luke, the "beloved doctor" (Col 4:14), is not a doctor of medicine but of law, and he defends Paul on trial in Rome. E. R. Goodenough suggests Acts is written to correct disturbing rumors about Paul,[10] and J. Munck shares the same opinion, insisting this is "the real purpose" (lviii).

These writers defend their view by pointing to the fact that not only does the Third Gospel present Christianity in favorable light but Acts presents Paul as a Roman citizen and proud of it, as he is also proud of the justice of the empire (Acts 16:37; 22:25). Paul preaches to the proconsul, Sergius Paulus, who becomes a convert (Acts 13:7,12). Roman officials declare Paul innocent: Gallio, proconsul in Achaia (Acts 18:12-16), and Felix and Festus, governors in Caesarea (Acts 26:31-32).[11] The tribune in Jerusalem (Acts 23:16-30) and several centurions treat Paul with respect and give him substantial freedom (Acts 22:26; 23:23-25), especially Julius of the Augustan Cohort, who guarded Paul during his voyage to Rome (Acts 27:1-28:16). Even in Rome Paul is simply under house arrest and is treated well (Acts 28:16). Thus Luke portrays Paul not only as innocent of any accusation but also as the model of Christianity's relationship with the empire.

It has also been suggested that what Luke gives us is not a defense of Christianity or of Paul but a defense of the empire before the Church. "Throughout his writings Luke has carefully, consistently, and consciously presented an *apologia pro imperio* to his Church" (Walaskay 64). According to some commentators, Luke neutralizes any anti-Roman material he finds in his sources and presents the value of being associated with the empire. Several authors suggest that in doing so, he anticipates many of the Fathers of the Church who seek imperial protection for the Church's missionary expansion and peaceful growth.

All three interpretations highlight the same basic purpose: to foster dialogue between the Church and the State. Both can live with each other; both can enrich each other.

Luke's New Pastoral Emphases

We have seen that Luke uses stylistic features and recurring themes to move his readers in the general direction of his pastoral concerns. He is above all a great spiritual guide and pastoral leader, and all that he does maintains an integrated emphasis on his pastoral goals. We have seen his pastoral sensitivity in calming his community's anxiety at the delay of the Lord's second coming. Likewise we have seen his care in adapting the message to his Gentile audience.

Luke's first pastoral emphasis is on rooting the faith in history. Some writers see Luke as a historian, and clearly he is concerned with presenting his work as historically reliable. Other writers believe he subordinates history to his theological interests and thus his work becomes historically unreliable. It seems hardly necessary to take opposite views on this issue. Luke reinterprets history, integrating the Church's time of waiting into God's plan of salvation history. He is always pastoral and evangelical. He is concerned about being historically accurate in order to give legitimate foundations for faith. He looks back at foundational events as "the basis and clue to his mission" (Hultgren 365), but his emphasis is not on the past but on how to live until the Lord returns. Luke challenges believers to look back themselves to see what was revealed so that they can look forward to how they should live. Always he is interested in showing how contemporary expressions of faith are based upon and legitimized by the historical events of Jesus' life and the life of the early Church.

Luke's second pastoral emphasis is on establishing a ministry of dialogue. Some writers stress Luke's attempts to establish a dialogue between Jews and Christians. While he seems in places to oppose the Jews, he elsewhere speaks so affirmingly that a few commentators believe he could have been a convert from Judaism. Some writers believe Luke presents God's epiphany to both Jews and Gentiles; they believe he presents God's mission as attained through Jesus, who is to be accepted as Lord by both Jews and Gentiles. Franklin puts it this way: "What Luke does is to try to account for Israel's disbelief in a way that does not cause a denial of her history and which leaves open her contact with God's promises" (114).[12] Other writers see Luke's dialogue between Jews and Gentiles and between Church and State as an attempt to take the pastoral rather than the polarizing approach.

Luke's third pastoral emphasis is on calling for unity in plurality. We have already seen that Acts presents unity between Peter and Paul and their respective focuses on the Jewish and Gentile parts of the Church. Luke also shows unity in plurality in the various forms of community structure: James governs Jerusalem and its surrounding province like a high priest and Sanhedrin; Antioch has charismatic elders; Paul governs many communities from a distance (sometimes delegating to co-workers); individual missionaries are sent by local churches; and Peter's authority seems local sometimes and universal other times. Cities like Jerusalem, Corinth, Antioch, and Ephesus have their own structures of authority. The story about the Jerusalem Council (Acts 15:1-35) also evidences Luke's desire to unite what could otherwise become divergent parts of the Church. Perhaps his pastoral concern for unity is best seen in his vision of the Church at Pentecost—a story that shows the reversal of the disunity of Babel.

The sense of unity Luke fosters is part of a fourth pastoral concern, namely, seeing the Christian story as an event of importance in world history. Luke begins with Jesus' ministry, locating it in the context of Caesar's world empire (Lk 3:1-2); as he begins Acts he refers to every known nation around the Mediterranean (Acts 2:5-11). In Acts the Church proclaims the Gospel in Jerusalem, the world's religious center, in Athens, the world's cultural center, and in Rome, the world's political center. In Acts the missionaries of the Church preach the good news to people of all classes, cultures, and countries. In his journeys Paul encounters the poor and the wealthy, the weak and the powerful, philosophers and the uneducated, the titled and the common people, civilians and the military, consuls, governors, and kings. He preaches to them all, convinced of the perennial and universal relevance of the Lord's message of salvation. Peter, the Jerusalem elders, and others such as Stephen adapt the Jewish-based message to the diaspora, the Gentiles, the Samaritans, and anyone else who is ready to receive it. In Acts the Church is ever ready and able to distinguish the heart of its message from secondary cultural trappings and is aware that Jesus' call is for the world.

Luke is both a great pastor and a great leader. He sees the changing conditions of the Church within the empire as a challenge to reformulate and reproclaim the perennial values of the message of the Lord. He reminds his audience that the end is not near, and with the death of the founding figures, everyone must courageously go forth, giving testimony to Jesus to the ends of the earth. For all such courageous missionaries he roots the faith in history, insists on a ministry of dialogue, calls for a catholic unity in pluralism, challenging us to be aware that this message is for all the world.

Theology of the Word

Theology of Ministry

Luke's interests are pastoral, which means we should use pastoral criteria to discern his major purpose. At first glance we see his two volumes are divided into time periods or areas of ministry. The Third Gospel presents the ministry of Jesus in Galilee, on the journey to Jerusalem, and in Jerusalem, with each period of ministry containing the same basic theological ideas.[13] Acts reports the great deeds of the apostolic heroes of the early Church.

Luke's Purpose in Writing Acts

It is not necessary to read all of Luke-Acts to catch the message. Each small section, easily absorbed in one reading session, describes a period of ministry with clearly delineated teachings and characteristics. In fact, each section contains the same major themes, format, and structure.

Acts parallels the ministry of the Church with Jesus' and then Paul's with Peter's. The Gospel shows Jesus calling forth others to ministry: the Twelve, the seventy-two, and individuals. Acts shows the Church likewise calling forth others to ministry: the seven deacons, Barnabas and Paul, Timothy, Mark, and several unnamed individuals. The Gospel's final section is Jesus' journey to Jerusalem to complete his ministry. Acts' final section is Paul's journey to Rome to "finish my course and the ministry that I received from the Lord Jesus" (Acts 20:24).

Luke inserts several explicit references to ministry. Peter tells Cornelius that the Holy Spirit anointed Jesus for ministry (Acts 10:38), and Jesus is aware that the Father sent him to minister to the world's needs (Lk 4:43). Luke refers to the Twelve as "apostles," "those who are sent," to emphasize their future ministry (Lk 6:13-16). Luke presents the ministry of the Twelve and of the seventy-two, and the latter represents the universal call to ministry (Lk 10:1-16). Luke gives us Jesus' ministry and the Church's continuation of that ministry.

Luke is dedicated to ministry and challenges others to that same dedication. His call to the Church is one of renewal through ministry—people learn about faith, then show their dedication to it by living in the service of others. His vision of faith implies participation in the missionary enterprise. Having presented the ministries of Jesus, he then stresses the dedication of the Twelve, the seventy-two, outstanding apostles, well-known disciples, lesser-known apostolic figures, and unnamed Church leaders, all of whom continue the

Lord's ministry to the ends of the earth. When Luke's story ends, the reader cannot help but respond, "Am I next? I'm also ready to continue this ministry of the Lord and his Church." In Luke's vision, the institutionalized ministers such as apostles and deacons are not the only ones who can claim to further the vision of the ministering Lord. According to Luke, every believer has this call, and the practice of constantly calling others to the ministry of the Word is precisely what leads to the successful spread of the good news.

Proclaiming the Word

The Word in Luke's writing is both personal and sacramental. Jesus is the prophet who both proclaims the message and embodies it. Furthermore, the Christian community not only proclaims the message but is sometimes identified with it: "in Acts Luke implies that logos...means more than the usual 'Christian message,' that somehow the meaning 'community' or 'People of God' is involved" (Kodell 511). Acts speaks of the glorification of Jesus and the glorification of the Word (Acts 3:13 and 13:48). By participating in the latter, the community participates in the life of Jesus himself, for response to his teachings leads to a relationship with him.

In the Third Gospel Jesus proclaims: "I came to bring fire to the earth, and how I wish it were already kindled!" (Lk 12:49). In Acts it is the Word that sets the earth on fire. In fact, Acts is divided into four sections by the same refrain repeated three times: "So the word of the Lord grew mightily and prevailed" (19:20; 6:7; 12:24). The four sections describe the nature and power of the Word[14] to draw others to faith and commitment. As Acts develops, we see that the great task of the Church is to spread the Word to the ends of the earth and to explain it so that all may understand (Acts 8:30-31). The theme of the Word—both personal and

Luke's Purpose in Writing Acts

powerful—is so important to Luke that one author claims, "Luke is as much a theologian of God's word as John" (Minear 141).

Luke's theology of the Word presented in Acts is anticipated in his Gospel. The story of the sower (Lk 8:5-15), in which "the seed is the Word of God" (Lk 8:11), describes four ways of receiving or rejecting this Word. Those who receive it well, the seeds that fall on good soil, "bear fruit with patient endurance" (Lk 8:15). The dialogue between the seed of the Word and believers represents a daily struggle with conversion, as people confront the way God thinks with the way they think. People can reject the Word, as many did when Paul preached, but once the Word finds welcome in a person's heart, it grows and multiplies, as if it has a personality of its own (Acts 6:7; 12:24). As Luke unfolds the history of the early Church, his presentation always "has a kerygmatic ring" to it; his history is "the witness of a believer which demands faith" (Betz 132). The history in Acts is kerygmatic testimony, the constant expansion of the Word of God.

Acts presents how the seed of the Word is spread. In the Gospel Luke changed the parable of the *sower* he inherited from Mark so that it became the parable of the *seed*. Luke understands that the Word, like seed, has the power of growth within it. The community's reception of the message—or the seed—manifests itself by bearing witness—or growing. Thus, when Luke describes the first major scattering of the seed, he refers to the spread of believers as a result of persecution: "Now those who were scattered went from place to place, proclaiming the word" (Acts 8:4). This scattering of believers refers to the spreading of the good news by the Christian community, who both embodies the Word and spreads the message.

As the Church spreads, so too does the Word. Salvation history is kerygmatic history—the growth and expansion of the Word, from Jerusalem, to Athens, to

Rome. The Word is not simply the content of the preaching of the early Church, nor the Church itself; the Word is Jesus Christ. As the Word moves away from the restrictions of Jerusalem, Jesus is extending his invitation of salvation to humanity.

The early Church prays that they can always preach the Word with boldness (Acts 4:29), and its leaders claim that they cannot give up their ministry of the Word (Acts 6:2). With the Church's cooperation, the Word grows on its own, gradually expanding as Jesus had hoped (Acts 6:7; 11:1; 12:24). Acts, then, recalls the victory of the Word to the ends of the earth.

Evangelization

Luke uses literary techniques for pastoral reasons. He uses different styles of Greek to appeal to different segments of his audience, and other stylistic features to create an atmosphere conducive to the reception of his message of faith. He skillfully integrates Gentile conventions into his proclamation of the good news and draws many to become open to its content through their comfort with its form. He structures his work on the theme of ministry, subdividing his second volume into periods of ministry. Among the major themes recurring in Acts, Luke emphasizes universal salvation, urges the need for religion to dialogue with society, and firmly gives priority to pastoral concerns.

The theology that emerges from Acts is a theology of ministry to the Word. Everything that Luke does moves the reader in this direction. One author expresses Luke's focus this way: "The discussion of the word of God is not a discussion of Jesus' teaching about his own teaching, but rather of Jesus' teachings about the preaching of the Christian church" (W. Robinson 132). Acts focuses on the Church's mission to spread the Word. We find Luke using the language of the Church regarding the community's responsibility and right to preach the Word. This ecclesiasticalization of evangelization need not be exaggerated, as if the institutional Church is taking control over every dimension of preaching. Rather, the real guide is the Holy Spirit.

Luke's intention is to present the Word in all its power in spite of all the social, political, and religious problems of his day,

> social forces which were continuously and cumulatively casting doubt on "the truth concerning the things of which you have been instructed," forces which were undermining confidence in the future of the Way and were destructive of resilient morale within the church (Minear 134).

When freed from prison, the apostles hear the Lord instructing them, "tell the people the whole message about this life" (Acts 5:20). They quickly learn that they must preach the Word no matter the cost (Acts 5:29), and they dedicate themselves to this ministry every day (Acts 5:42), even restructuring the community life to give themselves more freedom for this task (Acts 6:2-4). Scattered in persecution, they use the opportunity to preach the Word (Acts 8:4-6); left free, they travel the length and breadth of the country and surrounding regions, proclaiming the Word to Jews and Gentiles alike.

Everything that Luke does in his two volumes focuses on the challenge to his audience to "hear the word, hold it fast in an honest and good heart, and bear fruit with patient endurance" (Lk 8:15). Thus, his Gospel gives us Jesus' ministry to the Word, and Acts shows the Church's dedication to continuing that ministry. The universal call to participate in the community's work of evangelization is a task that must be fulfilled

Theology of the Word

by all believers with the boldness that is the gift of the Holy Spirit (Acts 4:29).

For Personal and Group Reflection

1. Luke makes every effort to adapt his message to the changing environments in which he finds himself. What do you think are the great successes and notable failures of the Church, locally and internationally, in its efforts to adapt to changing times and environments?

2. Luke sees the Church as a community that answers people's hopes and yearnings for fulfillment in life. What aspects of the Church do you find most fulfilling and enriching in your own life?

3. In Acts Luke presents his work, imitating interesting and effective means used by people in his own day, such as the journey narratives. How do you as a pastoral leader and minister use all the modern means available to proclaim the Gospel?

4. Journey is a key theme for Luke. How can parish leaders use the theme of journey for the educational formation of parishioners during the year?

5. Acts facilitates a dialogue between the Church and the State. What are the key areas of mutual interest today between Church and State? What are the major local political and social issues in which Church can be involved?

6. The writer of Acts constantly defends Christianity and its ministers before the challenges of other religious traditions and

state interference. What are the points in contemporary Christianity that you and your parish community could be defending?

7. In all that Luke does, he focuses on the primacy of the Word of God. Do you read the Scriptures regularly, using the Word as a basis for study, prayer, and reflection?

8. Faith in Acts involves participation in the mission and enterprises of the Church. How do you personally participate in Church life, and how do you facilitate the participation of others?

9. A sense of purpose permeates Luke's own commitment and his work for the faith. Are you motivated by a sense of purpose and commitment to the faith today?

10. Luke retains a series of key themes—major convictions regarding the values that ought to motivate the Church—which he repeats throughout his work. What are the key convictions that motivate your personal and parish life?

Chapter Four

Images of God in Acts

> It is not for you to know the times or periods that the Father has set by his own authority. But you will receive power when the Holy Spirit has come upon you; and you will be my witnesses in Jerusalem, in all Judea and Samaria, and to the ends of the earth (Acts 1:7-8).

In the Gospel of Luke, Jesus says that his mission is to proclaim the salvation of God to all humanity (Lk 3:6). Acts extends the knowledge of God to all nations. In his final address to the elders of Ephesus, Paul speaks for the whole Church when he says, "I did not shrink from declaring to you the whole purpose of God" (Acts 20:27). Evangelization is the great task of the Church, and the focus of proclamation is the revelation of God to humankind. Revelation is the core of all religion, as men and women seek to know and encounter God. Luke's portraits of the Father, Jesus, and the Holy Spirit in both the Third Gospel and Acts are wonderful syntheses that show the early Church's efforts to understand the implications of Jesus' teachings and extend his teachings to the world.

The God of Glory

Forgotten and Unrecognized

The great irony of the Gospel story is that most of the Jewish leaders and people who have been waiting for centuries for the coming of God's salvation do not recognize God's presence in Jesus. In fact, when Jesus is brought to trial before the Sanhedrin and asked to declare whether he is the Christ or not, he tells the High Priest, "If I tell you, you will not believe" (Lk 22:67). When hanging on the cross, Jesus is mocked by the people he came to save (Lk 23:35-38). After Pentecost, Peter, himself a Jew, condemns the ignorance and hard-heartedness of many of his fellow Jews, telling them, "You rejected the Holy and Righteous One...you killed the Author of life" (Acts 3:14-15). Jesus' own hidden life symbolizes the hiddenness of God's presence among a people who cannot recognize the arrival of the salvation for which they have hoped (Lk 2:39-40,51-52).

The apostles experience opposition from many of the Jews of the dispersion—those Jews scattered throughout the world—to their preaching of the message of God. Reactions from the Jews are often characterized by those Paul and Barnabas experienced in Pisidian Antioch:

> When the Jews saw the crowds, they were filled with jealousy; and blaspheming, they contradicted what was spoken by Paul. Then both Paul and Barnabas spoke out boldly, saying, "It was necessary that the word of God should be spoken first to you. Since you reject it and judge yourselves to be unworthy of eternal life, we are now turning to the Gentiles" (Acts 13:45-46).

The God of Glory

The inability on the part of many Jews to recognize the wonders of God in their midst make the missionaries' task very difficult. On the other hand, the opposition also persuades the missionaries to go to the Gentiles, an action which eventually leads to the world-wide proclamation of the revelation of God.

Gentiles, too, place obstacles in the way of the revelation. Their ignorance of religious truth leads them to see God in the magic of Simon, declaring, "This man is the power of God that is called Great" (Acts 8:10). Paul and Barnabas encounter similar ignorance in Lystra; when the Lycaonians see a miracle, they claim, "'The gods have come down to us in human form!' Barnabas they called Zeus, and Paul they called Hermes" (Acts 14:11-12). The local priest of Zeus wants to offer sacrifice to the apostles.

Paul confronts ignorance about God in his speech on the Areopagus in Athens. In this speech, given during his second missionary journey, he speaks to an audience of educated Gentiles who have no knowledge of Judaism. Paul deals specifically with the Epicurean and Stoic understandings of God, but on a more general level he shows the uselessness of the Gentiles' conception and worship of God. Wandering around Athens, Paul had seen an altar "to an unknown God"—a common practice among people of the first century. These people wanted to be sure they did not provoke the vengeance of any god, even one they did not know. Paul, the former zealous Pharisee, must have been overwhelmed and scandalized by the idolatry he saw. He challenges the Athenians' ignorance: "...he who is Lord of heaven and earth, does not live in shrines made by human hands....[W]e ought not to think that the deity is like gold, or silver, or stone, an image formed by the art and imagination of mortals" (Acts 17:24,29). Paul goes on to speak of natural revelation, teaching how God reveals self in creation, so that people "would search for God and perhaps grope for him and find him" (Acts 17:27). Paul suggests that, while people could have found God, and ought to have done so, many do not discover who God is. However, "God has overlooked the times of human ignorance, now he commands all people everywhere to repent" (Acts 17:30), for with the coming of Christ, the unknown God is now revealed.

Irruption of the Divine

With the coming of Jesus, God gives the world a season of refreshment (Acts 3:20), a time to see the wonders of the power of God. Gamaliel speaks of such a time, suggesting it could be so powerful no one would be able to withstand it (Acts 5:39). We see this breaking forth of divine power at the birth of Jesus, when the first group of Spirit-filled witnesses are gathered to proclaim the revelation of God's love (Lk 1). We see another great burst of this power and compassion at Pentecost, when all the nations of the earth are gathered to hear the good news (Acts 2:5-11), and Peter reminds them that they are witnessing the era of wonders that Joel prophesied (Acts 2:16-21).

Preachers like Peter and Stephen take pains to remind their audiences about God's interventions throughout salvation history (Acts 2:16-21; 7:2-53). Beginning with Pentecost, everyone—not only the Jews, but the whole world—must hear "about God's deeds of power" (Acts 2:11). Their vision includes the conviction that, ultimately, people can only know God through divine self-disclosure, and Jesus, the risen Lord, both explains and embodies the wonders of God's love for the world, calling people to appreciate the fact of God's involvement, interest, and desire for partnership with humanity.

Peter tells his audience that Jesus was "a man attested to you by God with deeds of power, wonders, and signs that God did through him among you" (Acts

2:22), and Luke understands Jesus' resurrection as the great act of God's interest in the world (Acts 2:24,32; 3:15,22,26; 4:10; 10:40; 13:30,34,37; 17:31; 26:8). Because of the resurrection, the world faces the compassion and interest of the all-powerful God, who shows the world the depth of divine involvement. Miracles worked by the apostles in Acts are like "mini resurrections" insofar as Luke sees them as participations in the powerful irruption of God's resurrectional power into human life: "With great power the apostles gave their testimony to the resurrection of the Lord Jesus, and great grace was upon them all" (Acts 4:33).

Ever-Present God

The early Church speaks of God as "Sovereign Lord" (Acts 4:24) and "Most High God" (Acts 16:17). This living God, a God of Glory (Acts 7:2), is creator of heaven and earth (Acts 4:24; 14:15; 17:24). In Acts God is involved in world history. Angels do God's bidding. They free Peter (Acts 5:19; 12:7), guide Philip (Acts 8:26), prepare Cornelius for conversion (Acts 10:3), and encourage Paul (Acts 27:23). Prophets in the Jewish Scriptures convey God's message (Acts 3:18-21), as do ministers in the early Church (Acts 6:7; 12:24; 13:5,46-49; 18:11).

Luke teaches that God is present in the great interventions in world history—in the past, in the present and in the future—especially through the divine plan. God determined and pre-ordained the events of world history (Acts 7:32-34; 17:26) and of salvation history, which culminated in the saving events of Jesus' life and death (Acts 2:23; 4:28; 10:42; 17:31).

In Acts Paul sees the whole of the evangelizing ministry of the Church as the continuation of the divine plan (Acts 20:27). God's power is present to the Church in miracles worked by the apostles (Acts 13:11; 19:11), in guidance given to missionaries (Acts 6:10; 27:23) as well as the favor of divine blessing (Acts 12:17; 14:25-27), in grace given to make people receptive to the message (Acts 10:15; 14:27), and in the challenge to spread the message to the Gentiles (Acts 11:17-18; 15:14). God not only directs the development of world history and the Church but also establishes the limits of time and the end of the world (Acts 1:7).

Luke emphasizes the idea of the divine plan with the use of compound words such as "fore-ordain" and "fore-knowledge," thereby indicating that God anticipates everything that happens. With the use of the verb "must," Luke shows how certain events happen because God wants them to; with the use of the phrase "as it is written," he shows that Scripture is fulfilled according to the plan of God. God is present in the events of history, in the fulfillment of the divine plan, and in the mission of Jesus. The apostles speak of sensing that God is present in their work (Acts 4:19), that God reads the hearts of men and women (Acts 1:24), and that our lives are acted out in the divine presence (Acts 10:31). Moreover, the power of God's salvific love is seen in the preaching of the Word and in the presence of the Holy Spirit (Acts 1:4). The apostles' experience in ministry convinces them that God is no longer hidden but clearly visible for all to see.

Our Father

Luke's Gospel speaks of God as Jesus' Father (Lk 1:32; 2:49; 10:21; 22:29; 23:34,46) and our Father (Lk 6:36; 11:2; 12:30); Acts presupposes this same distinction. God, who is a compassionate Father, listens to the prayers of the devout (Acts 10:31), shows no partiality in welcoming believers (Acts 10:34), and offers life-giving repentance and salvation to everyone (Acts 11:17-18; 14:27). The universal salvific will of the Father is part of the divine plan, and it is carried out in the ministry of Jesus (Acts 2:22; 3:18). The Father's love assures the fulfillment of the promises.

One of the great ways in which the Father fulfills the promises of Scripture is by sending the Holy Spirit on the Church (Acts 1:4-5; 2:33). The Father is also present in the powerful deeds witnessed in the early Church (Acts 2:11). Although the Father is referred to most commonly as "Lord" (between twenty-two and twenty-seven times—on a few occasions it is unclear whether Luke is referring to God or Jesus), believers do not respond to this power with fear, as if reacting to some unknown divinity. Rather, believers respond with praise and blessing, both in good times (Acts 2:47; 3:8) and in bad (Acts 4:21), always confident of the blessings of their loving Father. Although the end of the ages is determined by the Father (Acts 1:7), Luke tells the faithful that they need not approach this day with concern, for the Father is Savior (Acts 28:28) and source of universal salvation for humanity (Acts 11:17-18; 14:27). They do not earn the Father's saving grace; in fact, the Father has no need of human service (Acts 17:24-31). Luke insists that it is the Father's compassion for humanity which leads God to be near people in history and in all that they do each day.

Jesus, the Living Lord

Acts gives a rich and multifaceted portrait of Jesus. Luke's distinctive picture integrates many features found in the other Gospels. However, while "Luke...is the primary architect of the christological edifice of Acts" (MacRae 154), he also shows he is well aware of the christological diversity in the early Church. In his presentation of the person of Jesus, "He prefers to hold a large number of threads in his hand at once, introducing first one and then another...without allowing any one of them...to predominate over the rest" (Lampe 160). He weaves a synthesis of the beliefs of the early Church, not committing himself to any one of them. In fact, he seems to deviate from established models, such as those found in the other Gospels, in order to develop a christology of his own, made up of the insights of several traditions. Thus, at times his presentation is not harmonious; different portraits co-exist in the same section.[1]

The Sign and Sacrament of God

The Third Gospel presents the length of Jesus' ministry as approximately one year; Acts presents the involvement of Jesus in the life of the Church over a period of about thirty years. Luke seems to make a distinction between the way the disciples appreciated Jesus before the resurrection and their deep faith in him as Lord after the resurrection.[2]

The birth stories (Lk 1 and 2) are a prologue that anticipates the faith of the early Church, revealing Jesus as the Lord whom others will later recognize. Luke presents the baptism of Jesus as a creation story and portrays Jesus as the new Adam. In the central section of his ministry, the journey to Jerusalem (Lk 9:51-19:27), Jesus appears as the new Joshua, who leads his people into the promised land.

Describing Jesus' ministry, Peter says, "He went about doing good and healing all who were oppressed by the devil, for God was with him. We are witnesses to all that he did both in Judea and in Jerusalem" (Acts 10:38-39). During Jesus' ministry, the disciples see him as loyal to the Father, dedicated to his mission, sensitive and compassionate to people, and prophetically challenging to the standards of his day. The disciples are called to look beyond these events to appreciate the mystery of divine presence in Jesus.

Luke presents a "cavalcade of witnesses who can testify to the presence of the kingdom because they have discovered in Jesus the friend and champion of the sick, the poor, the penitent, the outcast, of women, Samaritans, and Gentiles" (Caird 37). In his ministry, Jesus is a sign or sacrament that points people in the direction of the mercy and goodness of God, challenging them to look beyond what they think they see to recognize the divine presence in the ministering Lord.

God's mercy and compassion in Jesus reaches its climax in his saving activity. Not only is Jesus the sign of God's grace, he is also the efficacious sacrament of God's salvation of humanity. Luke alone refers to Jesus as savior (Acts 5:31; 13:23) and sees this action of God in the whole activity of Jesus—not just in his death. This salvation continues in the ministry of the Church, through the power of the name, in the Church's preaching of "the word of his grace" and salvation (Acts 14:3; 20:24,32). Through all of this, Jesus is the "author of life" (Acts 3:15).

Jesus came to humanity "with deeds of power, wonders, and signs that God did through him" (Acts 2:22) because Jesus' life was above all lived in total obedience to the Father's will. Jesus is the instrument through whom the Father carries out the divine plan, anointed, consecrated, and attested by the Father for his ministry to the world (Acts 2:22; 4:27; 10:38). This obedience leads to Jesus' exaltation, as the Father glorifies him (Acts 3:13; 5:31), raises him (Acts 2:22-24,30-32; 3:15,26; 4:10; 5:30; 10:38-39), makes him Lord (Acts 2:34-36), and appoints him judge of the living and the dead (Acts 10:42; 17:31).

Acts presents Jesus' life as the beginning of a new era of God's creative interventions in the world. Jesus himself is the fulfillment of all God's promises, the instrument of God, and our savior. During his ministry, Jesus is the sign that points people in the direction of God, and in the resurrection he is the effective

Images of God in Acts

instrument of God's salvation for the world. In Acts Jesus is Lord and Christ, the Author of Life, and the object of the Church's faith.

The Servant of the Lord

In Bethlehem the angel brings "good news of great joy for all the people" (Lk 2:10) and proclaims Jesus as son of David, savior, and Messiah. In Jerusalem, after the events of Pentecost, Peter declares a season of refreshment with the coming of Jesus (Acts 3:20), the Lord and Messiah. Luke presents Jesus as a new Joshua in the journey narrative, and as a new Elijah in his reactions to rejecting Samaritans (Lk 9:54) and in his ascension (Lk 24:50-51). However, Jesus is more than a prophet who calls the people to God: he is the risen Lord (Acts 10:37-43), the stone rejected by the builders who becomes the cornerstone of the whole building (Acts 4:11).

Isaiah prophesies the coming of a suffering servant of the Lord. His four songs (Isa 42:1-7; 49:1-7; 50:4-9; 52:13-53:12) describe the life and sufferings of a mysterious figure who is chosen by God and gives his life for the benefit of others. The first song describes the servant's call, the second his mission, the third the kind of life he lives, and the fourth the bitter suffering he endures on behalf of others. Luke uses the word "servant" to describe Jesus in context of his ministry and suffering, which recalls Isaiah's servant. Thus the people gather together against God's holy servant (Acts 4:27), but God protects and raises up his servant (Acts 3:26). Now signs and wonders are worked in the name of the servant (Acts 4:30). When Philip encounters the Ethiopian eunuch, he explains to him the fourth servant song of Isaiah, showing it is fulfilled in Jesus (Acts 8:32-35).

Luke has been criticized for subordinating Jesus to the Father.[3] However, it seems unrealistic to presume believers could jump from the rigorous monotheism of Judaism to the Christian understanding of Trinity. There were stages and levels of understanding in the communities' grasp of the kerygma. In Luke's Gospel, human beings do not refer to Jesus during his ministry with titles of "Lord," "Son," "Bestower of the Spirit," "Son of Man," or "Savior"—these titles are used by angels and demons. But in Acts all of these titles are part of the mature faith of the early Church.[4]

One writer refers to six stages in Luke's presentation of Jesus as the servant of the Lord, with each stage represented by a key word.[5] Jesus' journey to his passion and death is an *exodus* as it was for the Chosen People, God's servant Israel (Lk 9:31). After his passion, Jesus *entered into* his glory (Lk 24:26). Following forty days of post-resurrection appearances and teaching to his apostles, Jesus was *received up* into heaven (Acts 1:2,11,22; 2:34). In heaven Jesus *sits at the right hand* of the Father (Lk 20:42; 22:69; Acts 2:34). As the deacon Stephen is put to death, he sees Jesus *standing up* at God's right hand, getting up as if something is about to begin (Acts 7:55-56). Finally Jesus *will come again* as final judge (Lk 9:26; 12:36-38; 18:8; 21:27).

Luke presents Jesus from his birth to his second coming. Luke begins by portraying Jesus as a servant who acts on behalf of God and ends by portraying Jesus' activity as identical to God's.

The Living Lord of All

Luke links in inseparable unity the historical Jesus and the risen Lord. Luke's two-volume work hinges on the fact of the resurrection. The resurrection is anticipated in passages that give the passion predictions, seen in the stories of the empty tomb, and affirmed in references to post-resurrection appearances. Peter tells the Pentecost crowd that it was impossible for death to keep its hold on Jesus (Acts 2:24). Freed from death and raised in glory, Jesus is recognized by the early Church as "the Author of life" (Acts 3:15) and the "Lord of all" (Acts 10:36).

Luke's infancy narrative serves as a synthesis of the Church's creed. It is as if the infancy narrative summarizes the person whom the faith-filled Church will later recognize Jesus to be. In those pages Luke often uses several titles of Jesus at the same time: in the angels' proclamation (Lk 2:11) and in Zechariah's and Simeon's canticles (Lk 1:69; 2:29-32). He thus shows that Jesus fulfills several strands of tradition at the same time, for he is the full and complete instrument of God, Messiah in a greater way than anyone expected.

Luke does not allow humans to use titles for Jesus during the ministry, but that changes in Acts. In Acts, Jesus is above all Christ and the Lord. He is the Messiah (Acts 2:31,36; 8:5; 17:3), the Righteous One (Acts 22:14-15), and the final prophet that Moses had promised would come (Acts 3:22-23; 7:37; Deut 18:15). He is the eschatological judge and agent of redemption, known as the Son of Man (Acts 7:56). Moreover, the apostles proclaim that Jesus is Son of God (Acts 9:20; 13:33), who bestows the Holy Spirit on the Church (Acts 2:33; 16:7). The faithful declare that Jesus is "Leader and Savior" (Acts 5:31), the culminating promise of salvation history—a Savior for Israel (Acts 13:23) and for everyone in the world (Acts 13:47; 28:28).

In the Septuagint version of the Jewish Scriptures, the word "Lord" *(kyrios)* is the Greek translation of "Yahweh," the sacred name of God. In Acts the author uses the word indiscriminately of both God and Jesus. "The conclusion appears to be that in the usage of Acts at any rate the title implied that the lordship belonging to God had been transferred in part to Jesus" (Marshall, *Luke*, 166). The early community soon changed "Christ Jesus" to "Lord Jesus," thus expressing their confession in the lordship of Jesus.

Christ and the Church

The links between Jesus and the Church are always in Luke's mind throughout the writing of the two volumes; the interests he has in Acts are already in his thoughts when writing the Gospel. Luke devotes much of the Gospel to Jesus' preparing the apostles for their future mission in the Church through his guidance, teaching and examples of ministry.

Stephen is the Church's first martyr, and his death leads to the spread of the Gospel (Acts 8:1,4). Luke is the first to suggest that the blood of the martyrs is the seed of the Church. As Stephen is stoned, he sees the heavens open and the Son of Man standing up in readiness to help the world (Acts 7:56). In Acts Jesus is eager to support and be present to his Church. In fact Jesus teaches Paul that when the Church is persecuted Jesus himself feels it (Acts 9:4). Jesus is not inactive in heavenly glory; he is still the savior in everyday life (Acts 4:12), the leader and ruler (Acts 5:31), the universal judge (Acts 10:42), and the one who forgives sin (Acts 13:38).

Luke is the only evangelist to explicitly portray Jesus' exaltation through an ascension story, and he uses the event as the hinge between the Gospel and Acts. The ascension at the end of the Gospel is a no-frills account that focuses on the glorification and exaltation of the Lord (Lk 24:30-53). The account in Acts, the "ecclesiastical ascension," gives the implications of Jesus' departure for the life of the early Church (Acts 1:6-11). The end of the story of Jesus is the beginning of the story of the Church, and the second account establishes the evangelical program for the Church. It stresses the presence of the Lord to his Church and the latter's mission in his name. The ascension ends the period of post-resurrection appearances and affirms that Jesus is now present to the Church in new and more powerful ways: in his Word, Spirit, name, preaching, signs and

Images of God in Acts

wonders, visions, community, and the Breaking of Bread.

Peter and the apostles work miracles in the name of Jesus; Peter heals the lame man at the Beautiful Gate of the Temple (Acts 3:1-10). Peter claims that the miracles that Jesus worked in his ministry acted as his credentials (Acts 2:22); the miracles serve a similar function for the Church in Acts. These miracles are signs of the power of the risen Lord and prove the apostles' claim that Jesus is truly risen. They witness to the resurrection and continue the resurrectional power of God. Thus, Luke states, "With great power the apostles gave their testimony to the resurrection of the Lord Jesus" (Acts 4:33). The miracles, seen as "mini resurrections," are meant to imply that the same power that raised Jesus to new life now raises these people to new life.

In Judaism the "name" refers to reality. One of the most important ways in which Jesus remains present to the Church is through the power of his name. Through the faithful invocation of the reality of who Jesus is known to be, Jesus is present. When converts become members of the Church, they are baptized in the name of Jesus (Acts 2:38; 8:16; 10:48; 19:5; 22:16), for the Church is aware that forgiveness of sin is found in Jesus (Acts 10:43; 22:16) and that "there is no other name under heaven given among mortals by which we must be saved" (Acts 4:12). The apostles taught in the name of Jesus (Acts 4:18; 5:28,40), preaching the power of his name (Acts 8:12; 9:15,27). Church leaders heal the sick in the name of Jesus (Acts 3:6,16; 4:10; 9:34), work miracles in his name (Acts 4:30), and exorcise in his name (Acts 16:18). So powerful is the believers' sense of Jesus' presence in his name, they are willing to suffer (Acts 5:41) and die for the sake of this name (Acts 21:13).

The immediate effect of the death and resurrection of Jesus is that people are called to turn from their wickedness and receive the forgiveness of God (Acts

3:26; 5:31). Jesus' redemptive death makes him "Author of life" (Acts 3:15) and savior (Acts 5:31). Individuals find this forgiveness and new life within the community of faith that gathers around Jesus. Jesus acquired his Church through his own blood (Acts 20:28). Now, in Acts, the Lord is present to his Church through its ministry, through visions (Acts 7:54-56; 9:1-16,27; 22:6-16,17-21; 23:11; 26:12-18), through the inspiration of the Holy Spirit (Acts 1:2,8; 2:33,38; 16:6-7), and when supporting his ministers in their trials (Acts 5:19; 9:16; 12:7).[6]

The Church's ministers dedicate their lives to the cause of our Lord Jesus Christ (Acts 15:26) and model their lives and deaths on Jesus (Acts 7:60 and Lk 23:34; Acts 27:1-28:16 and Lk 9:51-19:27). Luke portrays the apostles as doing the same kind of things Jesus did, working similar miracles, and suffering in ways Jesus did. Their lives, modeled on his, are a further way in which Jesus is present to the Church.

Jesus is sign and sacrament of God's compassion and love. He is the Suffering Servant of the Lord, who through his life and death becomes the Living Lord of all. Now he remains present to his Church in signs and wonders, in the power of his name, in the reconciling ministry of the Church, and in the examples of his disciples.

The Holy Spirit—the Father's Promise

Gift of God

Luke has often been called the evangelist of the Holy Spirit. He refers to the Holy Spirit fifty-four times, more than all other evangelists combined. Most of these references (forty-one) are in Acts. While Matthew in his Gospel speaks of the good things that God gives to those who ask (Mt 7:11), Luke changes it to affirm that the greatest gift of God is the Holy Spirit (Lk 11:13). The action of the Spirit is seen in the inspiration of Scripture that foretold the coming of the Messiah (Acts 1:16; 4:25; 28:25), and it climaxes in readying the community of *anawim* ("the poor ones of the Lord") to accept the coming of the Messiah. In Acts the Spirit prepares believers for the birth of the Church at Pentecost (Acts 2:1-4).

The coming of the Holy Spirit on the disciples is not the result of any activity on the part of the recipients. They are told to wait in Jerusalem until they are clothed in the Spirit of the Lord (just as Elisha was clothed with the spirit of Elijah [2 Kings 2:10]). Moreover they are told that the event will happen "not many days from now" (Acts 1:5), so they hardly have time to prepare.

The Spirit is a gift for all believers, not just some of them. The possession of the Holy Spirit confirms baptism and constitutes the Church (Acts 8:4-24). When the Spirit is recognized to be present in a person, the Spirit demands that the person be baptized into the Church if he or she has not already been (Acts 10:44-48). Making people aware of the gift of the Spirit is a responsibility for the whole Church: Peter (Acts 2:14-37), John (Acts 8:4-24), Philip (Acts 8:26-40), Ananias (Acts 9:17-19), and Paul (Acts 19:1-7).

In Acts this gift, experienced especially at Pentecost, is seen as the fulfillment of Jewish Scriptures. The coming of the Spirit fulfills the expectation that the eschatological community of God will one day be filled with the messianic Spirit (Acts 2:17-21; Isa 44:3-5). The Spirit is poured out on believers who commit themselves to the name of Jesus (Acts 2:33) and through them is offered to all the world (Acts 2:38-39). The Holy Spirit is the gift of God that gives life and unity to the Church and is the dynamic force for the Church's ministry.

The Spirit is given to enrich the Church for preaching (Acts 2:4; 4:31; 6:10), witnessing (Acts 4:8; 5:32; 13:9), choosing (Acts 6:1-7; 11:17; 13:2) and directing the activity of ministers (Acts 8:29,39; 11:12; 13:4; 16:6-7), prophesying (Acts 11:28; 21:4,11), and supporting the community (Acts 9:31; 13:52). This gift is so necessary to the Church that Luke identifies the gift of the Spirit with the Church (Acts 5:3,9).

Revealer of Truth

The Holy Spirit is the inspiration for the revealed Word of God (Acts 1:16; 4:25; 28:25). Moreover, the Holy Spirit guides Jesus in every step of his early ministry (Lk 4:1-14) and in the choice of the Twelve (Acts 1:2). After Pentecost, the ever-present Spirit guides the Church in its understanding and preaching of the truth of Jesus (Acts 2:4; 4:8). Soon the apostles see their total dependence on the revealing presence of the Holy Spirit and their need to be ever obedient to the Spirit's inspiration. They even insist that when they are responsive to the Spirit their witnessing is identical to the Spirit's challenge (Acts 5:32). The Spirit not only initiates and directs the Church's mission (Acts 8:29-39; 10:19) but explains in detail what needs to be done (Acts 11:12).

The discernment of the Council of Jerusalem is guided by the Spirit (Acts 15:28), as is the decision to expand the mission to the Gentiles (Acts 11:12). The latter is a very important decision for the early Church, and the Holy Spirit prepares the leaders, gradually revealing to them the need for this refocusing of the Church's ministry (Acts 10:17-21; 11:12; 13:46-52; 15:28; 28:23-28).

The Spirit works through the evangelization of disciples (Acts 16:6-7; 20:22-23; 21:4), empowering them in the proclamation of the Word (Acts 2:4; 4:8; 6:5; 7:55; 9:17; 11:24; 13:4), and giving them boldness to perse-

Images of God in Acts

vere in spite of oppression (Acts 4:8,31; 5:32). The Spirit directs the course of the Church's evangelization. Opposition to the teaching of the Church is seen as opposition to the Holy Spirit (Acts 7:51). The Church's loyalty to the guidance of the Holy Spirit guarantees that their preaching is an authentic continuation of the preaching of Jesus.[7]

Guardian of the Church

In Acts Luke parallels the ascension of Jesus to the Father's side and the resultant gift of the Spirit with Moses' ascent of Mount Sinai and the gift of the Law. For Luke the Spirit is to the Christian what the Law is to the Jew: the constant rule by which believers measure their lives. Rather than having a law to guide them, believers have a power deep within them. Thus, the Spirit fulfills what Jeremiah foretold—that God would place a law deep within people's hearts (Jer 31:31-34).

This guiding presence is not something individualistic; there is a deep union between the Spirit and the community. The Spirit enables a common witnessing to the Gospel, the growth in a common faith, the training of apostles with a common vision, the awakening of a shared desire to go to the Gentiles.

> This implies an association of the Spirit with the community amounting in some sense to identity: it is the Spirit that informs and animates the community, which indeed, apart from the Spirit would not be a community but an aggregate of individuals (Bruce, "Holy Spirit in Acts," 173).

When the apostles make a decision, they claim it is the Holy Spirit's decision (Acts 15:28).

The Spirit guides the apostles (Acts 1:2) and gives them courage to be faithful to the message (Acts 2:4). In fact, the expression "full of the Holy Spirit" becomes Acts' characteristic way of referring to Christian leaders: Peter (Acts 4:8), Stephen (Acts 6:5), Barnabas (Acts 11:24), and Paul (13:9).[8] When the Church appoints deacons, it seeks people who are filled with the Holy Spirit (Acts 6:3) because their ministry was to be based on the prophetic gifts of the Spirit, not on human wisdom. "Lucan style is characterized by these 'plenitude formulas' in which is described fullness of the Spirit, of power, of grace, or of joy. All suggest that the Spirit is the cause of this fullness" (Navone, *Themes,* 59).

The Spirit guards the Church in practical ways, specifying where ministry should be focused (Acts 8:29; 10:19; 13:4) and where it should not (Acts 16:6-7). Often the Spirit guards and guides the missionaries of the Church (Acts 8:29; 19:21). At times the Spirit speaks through communities' inspiration (Acts 20:22-23; 21:4,11). The presence of the Spirit brings consolation (Acts 9:31), joy (Acts 13:52), and the spirit of prophecy (Acts 11:28; 19:6; 21:11).

At first the involvement of the Spirit is spontaneously manifested through any believer, but gradually the Spirit is given through the leaders of the Church (Acts 8:17; 19:6). Furthermore, the Church itself comes to be seen as entrusted to the leaders by the Holy Spirit (Acts 20:28). At the beginning of Acts, the Spirit is given to the Church and constitutes the Church; by the end of Acts the Church gives the Spirit.

Witness to the Lord

Jesus told his disciples that when they received the Holy Spirit they would become his witnesses (Acts 1:8). The conviction that the Spirit is the source of witness permeates the whole of Acts. Jesus himself begins his ministry when anointed with the Spirit and with

Images of God in Acts

power (Acts 10:37-38), and Jesus promises the Church that same power (Acts 1:8). The power of the Spirit is not the power of great deeds (Acts 8:20-22) but the power to witness (Acts 6:8). When describing the preaching of the Church's ministers, Luke often says they were filled with the Holy Spirit (Acts 13:9) as Jesus was in his ministry (Lk 4:1).

The Holy Spirit makes believers witnesses to Jesus. "For Luke, Jesus is not a figure of the past, but the living Lord. The Spirit is not the substitute for the living Jesus but the witness to the fact that he lives and is the present Lord" (Franklin 46). The Spirit equips the Church to give authentic witness to Jesus, for the Spirit is the Spirit of Jesus (Acts 16:7). Marshall concludes, "The Holy Spirit as such is not Luke's main theme....[I]t is in witness that the Holy Spirit is central" (Marshall, *Luke*, 92).

Acts is the story of the Holy Spirit because Acts is the history of the Church's evangelization. When that evangelization is rejected, ministers assert that it is the Holy Spirit who has been rejected (Acts 5:3; 7:51).

The God of Glory, forgotten by many, has broken into our world as the ever-present Father. Jesus directs the world to God and is the Servant who becomes the Living Lord of all. He is now present to the Church in multiple ways, none greater than through the gifts of revelation, guidance, and power to witness that come from his Spirit.

For Personal and Group Reflection

1. We place obstacles in the way of knowing God more, we remain in ignorance of God's ways, and God progressively becomes unknown to us and forgotten. What practical steps can we take to learn

more about God and establish a deeper relationship with God?

2. The resurrection is the wonderful irruption of the divine into human history, an irruption that continues in the "mini resurrections" of every believer's life. What are the ways in which you have experienced God's presence to you in the last year?

3. God, ever present in the ministries of the prophets of old, is equally present in the lives of today's ministers, who continue the prophetical role for today's world. How do you, your parish, and its various teams nurture opportunities in which God's presence is constantly experienced?

4. God develops world history, and the divine plan is at work all the time. Do you realize that you are participating in the grand plan of God? How do you show this awareness in the ways you live and minister?

5. Luke presents Jesus as the sign and sacrament of God's loving presence to the world. In what ways are your own family and parish signs and sacraments of God's loving presence to the world?

6. In Luke's Gospel, believers, including chosen disciples, only gradually get to know who Jesus is. In Acts, the Church's faith is clear and mature. What tensions do you experience between the clear and mature faith of the Church that you teach to others and the daily struggles of faith?

Images of God in Acts

7. The ascension shows that Jesus is continually present to the Church, and Luke shows that believers experience Jesus' presence in the Word, Spirit, his name, preaching, signs and wonders, community and the Eucharist, to mention a few. Where do you and your parish encounter Jesus' presence today?

8. One of the ways in which Jesus is present to the Church in Acts is through dedicated ministers. How do you believe that you portray the presence of Jesus to others? What additional ways of portraying that presence can you think of?

9. The Holy Spirit, revealer of truth, guarantees the authenticity of preaching. How do ministers and parishes guarantee believers that what they teach is an authentic expression of faith?

10. In Acts there is some tension between the spontaneous gift of the Holy Spirit to believers and the conveying of the Spirit through the channels of the institutional Church. How is that tension experienced today?

Chapter Five

Life in the Early Church

> They devoted themselves to the apostles' teaching and fellowship, to the breaking of bread and the prayers (Acts 2:42).

Even during the time of Jesus' ministry, disciples became aware that they formed a special group around Jesus, faithful to his teachings and to each other. All the writings of the New Testament evidence this conviction. In the early years, believers developed common credal statements and expressions of community life, as they together awaited for what they believed would be the immediate return of the Lord.

All the Gospels were written after the Church realized that the Lord's second coming would not be immediate. This delay was one of the two great crises in the early Church: If Christ would soon return, why must the Church exist at all? Each Gospel struggles to answer the question about what believers should do and how they should live in the time of waiting.

More than any other writer, Luke gives detailed descriptions of the early Church and also reflects on what he understands to be the nature of this community of faith. Writing Acts around the year 85, he looks

Life in the Early Church

back over fifty or sixty years and asks: What is unique about the Church's origins? What are the characteristics of its life that need to be repeated in each successive generation if believers are to faithfully express what is essential to this communal manifestation of faith? In the Third Gospel Luke stresses the place of Jesus in redemptive history, and in Acts he addresses the place of the Church in the redemptive plan of God.

The Nature of the Church

Key Lukan Concepts

Jesus did not found the Church, but as the Third Gospel shows, he does challenge his followers and initiate a process that leads to the establishment of a community of faith. Founded on Jesus, the rejected cornerstone (Acts 4:11), this community would be open to everyone throughout the world, a channel of God's grace and a place in which to find the Lord's salvation.

The early Church's preaching implied that to believe the good news meant to accept membership in a community; in Acts salvation means belonging to the community of the saved. Luke expands the horizons of our faith by showing us not only what God has done in Jesus' life and death but also what God continues to do in Jesus through the Church. In Acts, Luke presents the principal issues that are fundamental to an understanding of Church. His interpretation of early Church history tells us a little about what the origins of the Church were like—for he does try to give us some history of the first three decades—but more precisely he presents a vision of what the Church ought to be. He presents the apostolic Church as a paradigm for Church life in every generation.

The Nature of the Church

Luke sees the Church as the people of God, the community that now fulfills the hopes of Israel. In the course of his Gospel, Luke presents several parables that emphasize his view regarding the inadequacy of Judaism to fulfill the design of God. Some of the parables were exclusive to Luke and others he selected from the synoptic tradition.[1] He presents the Christian community as the successor to Israel, "the descendants of the prophets and of the covenant" (Acts 3:25). He applies to the Church concepts traditionally reserved to Israel: the remnant (Acts 2:47) and the heritage of Abraham (Acts 3:25). In fact, Luke suggests "that the Christians are the true Israel and that the break with Judaism was not caused by Christians, but by Jews" (Hengel 63).

Luke sees the Church as the new *qahal* or assembly of the Lord's people (Acts 2:21-36; 5:11; 8:1,3; 9:31; 11:22,26). He speaks frequently about the coming of the kingdom, right up to the eve of Jesus' passion, insisting that it is still not here (Lk 19:11; 22:18; 23:42). After the passion he speaks as if the kingdom is now present (Lk 24:26; Acts 1:3). Luke is convinced that the hopes of Israel to be the beneficiaries of God's promises are now found in the new assembly of God's people, the Church. The opportunity to enter the kingdom is now available to everyone in the preaching of the good news.

Luke also understands the Church to be the eschatological Zion (Acts 2:39), the community that God promised would be established in the final age (Acts 2:17,22,39,43). Jesus is the eschatological prophet foretold by Moses (Acts 2:22-23; 7:37), and Peter declares that signs and wonders about which Joel prophesied are manifested at Pentecost. Acknowledged as the messianic community, the Church is a new creation, belonging to a new era of God's saving work in the world. Luke begins Acts with a creation epic, Pentecost, which reminds readers of the Spirit, who hovers over

Life in the Early Church

the waters at the beginning of creation, of the reversal of the world confusion at Babel, and of the covenant of Sinai. Pentecost is not an end but a beginning of a new dynamism in the Church, a new presence of Jesus to his Church.

The Church is the community created by the pouring out of the Holy Spirit on the day of Pentecost (Acts 2:1-21). The Father sends the promised gift (Lk 24:48-49; Acts 1:5), the pledge and anticipation of salvation, to the Church at each of the foundational experiences of local communities: Jerusalem (Acts 2:1-4), Samaria (Acts 8:14-17), the Gentile Church at Cornelius' house (Acts 10:44), and Ephesus (Acts 19:6). We have already seen that the Holy Spirit not only gives birth to the Church but sustains and guides it at every moment, empowering it for mission, witness, preaching, and giving consolation (Acts 9:31).

Universal Salvation in the Church

Only in Luke's Gospel does John the Baptist anticipate the universal salvation that Jesus brings, claiming that with his coming "all flesh shall see the salvation of God" (Lk 3:6). When Simeon welcomes the new-born Christ, he declares him to be "a light for revelation to the Gentiles and for glory to your people Israel" (Lk 2:32). Before his ascension, Jesus entrusts to his Church this same mission of universal salvation (Acts 1:8). At the birth of the Church at Pentecost, Peter tells the crowd that "the promise is for you, for your children, and for all who are far away, everyone whom the Lord our God calls to him" (Acts 2:39).

Luke portrays the Father as Lord of history and this portrayal leads to practical pastoral implications. The focus of Acts is essentially universal. In Acts the Church breaks the closed circle of Judaism and becomes open to universality, a vision based on the ministry of Jesus. Peter's statement to the Gentile Cornelius, "I truly understand that God shows no partiality, but in every nation anyone who fears him and does what is right is acceptable to him" (Acts 10:34-35), is a lesson Luke also learned, for he shows notable openness and tolerance toward all groups and individuals: Samaritans, public sinners, and Roman officials, for example.

Luke drives a wedge between the Jewish leaders and "the people" of Jerusalem, the latter being a term he often uses later to refer to the Church. In relation to the leaders, Luke seems to be more positive toward the Pharisees but negative to the Sadducees (perhaps because the former were in power when he wrote Acts, and as usual he tries to maintain some hope of dialogue). Luke's "two-volume history would have offered [Jewish Christians] a renewed sense of their identity as God's people" (Juel 117).[2] Luke omits Mark's account of the tearing of the Temple curtain, and he is never critical of Jews who give importance to the Temple, cult, and Law. He seems ready to integrate into his universal vision any values that people hold dear, provided they do not clash with dedication to Christ.

Luke also speaks positively of Samaritans in his Gospel (Lk 10:29-37; 17:11-19) and describes the origins and development of Samaritan Christianity (Acts 8:14-25). Some commentators suggest that Stephen's speech, based on the Samaritan Pentateuch, is a Samaritan interpretation of salvation history. The Samaritans are not isolated by the early Church but drawn into its membership through faith in the Lord.

Guided by the Holy Spirit, Philip converts a black African from ancient Ethiopia, possibly a proselyte preparing for Judaism. The story becomes another step in Luke's movement to the universal significance of the Church's mission. Ethiopia was certainly the ends of the earth in New Testament times.

As was discussed earlier, the Church's major pastoral decision was the commitment to welcome Gentiles. Jesus affirms the devotion and faith of a Gentile centurion (Lk 7:1-10); Peter bar Jonah, imitating his own namesake (Jon 4:10-11), learns what the vision of God implies (Acts 11:9) and proclaims salvation to the Gentiles (Acts 10:1-48). However, Cornelius is led to belief in Jesus from his devotion to Judaism—a view that several in the early Church considered normative.

At first the Church seems to have shown some reluctance to accept the Gentiles. The problem is apparently settled in chapters 10-11 and then is reopened in chapter 15. Paul continues to face opposition from some Church leaders to his work among the Gentiles up to the end of his ministry.

The Church's openness to the Gentiles seems to have led to nothing more than a more liberal proselytizing policy for a Jewish-centered Church in Jerusalem (Acts 15:14-18); eventually, however, this openness leads to a new way of understanding the Church as a community distinct from Judaism. Around the year 48, the Jerusalem Council established guidelines for the acceptance of Gentiles, but after the Council the missionaries quickly abandoned these restrictions. Acts is the geographical and theological journey to the Gentile Church; in it, the missionaries treat all people with respect and appreciation for their own backgrounds— bringing all the season of refreshment about which Peter spoke (Acts 3:20-21).[3]

Acts presents reasons for all humanity to hope; Luke makes the offer of salvation present and visible for all people of good will. Under the guidance of the Lord's vision, Peter actually changes his mind from opposition to Gentile membership to being the initiator of the Gentile mission. Peter becomes the model for other Church leaders; he is able to adapt imaginatively to the changed circumstances of the Church's mission.[4] The Church's universal vision, which enables it to realize that Gentiles need not observe Jewish laws for full membership in the Church, allows it to dialogue with people who have been marginalized by Judaism, such as the Samaritans and Gentiles.

In Acts the Church is part of the great drama of salvation, and its universal mission is a lesson for the Church in every generation.

Community in History

Luke gives many indications of historical accuracy, for example, knowledge of local details and aspects of Roman politics and administration. He clearly wants his work to be viewed as a history—provided of course we understand history in his way and not ours. However, neither historical nor geographical accuracy are Luke's primary interests. He is writing history from the perspective of faith; for Luke all history is the history of salvation. Moreover, he uses geography symbolically. Truthful in those things that are necessary for salvation, he often uses previously existing Jewish or Hellenistic stories to convey the truths of which he is convinced.

Some writers, like Rudolf Bultmann and his followers, have played down the historical value of episodes used by Luke, and they have criticized what they think is Luke's practice of neglecting Jesus' eschatological message in favor of access to grace through the Church. They believe that Jesus' primitive proclamation consists of a call to immediate repentance and a decision to find salvation in Jesus the Lord. These writers consider that Luke substitutes the Church with its authority, sacraments, teachings, and ecclesiastical offices for the immediate call to conversion to the Lord. By the time Luke finishes Acts, they suggest, he presents an early version of the Roman Catholic Church. Criticized for this "early catholicism," Luke is seen by these writers as having betrayed the original teachings of Jesus.[5]

Some critics of the above position do not see history and eschatology as opposites but see eschatology as bound up with history. They see history as God's means of achieving the divine purpose. History is the drama of world redemption. Luke's doctrinal presentation is rooted in history—a history of God's saving interventions in human history, not a chronicle of events.[6]

For Luke, Pentecost is an eschatological event and leads to the Church's mission. He does not abandon eschatology; rather he refers to both a delayed, futurist eschatology and an imminent eschatology. The former helps his community avoid false apocalypticism (believing in some cataclysmic end to the world), and the latter laxity (in which people become unfaithful because no end is expected).[7]

Luke's response is that of a pastoral leader. "Thanks to him, the early Church did not collapse into an hysterical futurist eschatology" (van Stempvoort 42). Luke reinterprets eschatology rather than reduces it. He helps the Church adapt a new outlook on the time of the Lord's return. He presents God's grace breaking into the world in three ways: in the promise of the Jewish Scriptures, in the fulfillment of the Jewish Scriptures through Jesus' life and death, and in universal salvation made possible through the ministry of the Church. Salvation, promised of old, revealed in Jesus, is now proclaimed by the Church.

Luke presents the eschatological events of Jesus over a period of time so that he gradually leads the community to appreciate what took place in the passion and resurrection of Jesus; thus he gradually explains to them and they gradually appreciate the nature of the Holy Spirit and the Church. One writer says: "There is no either/or in primitive Christianity between eschatology and salvation-history. The eschatological events form part of salvation-history" (Marshall, *Luke*, 109). Another writer, commenting on Luke's defense of the faith, says:

> History, apology, and eschatology form interrelated components of Luke's theology. If history describes where the community has been and eschatology describes where it is going, then apology describes where the community is now (Walaskay 1).

Luke locates Jesus' salvation in the Church, and when people accept the Lord's invitation they are "added" to the Church (Acts 2:41,47; 5:14). People who seek salvation are told they will be instructed by Church leaders (Acts 11:14; 16:30-31).

> Luke sees the salvation of the individual as indissolubly connected with the Church, since only through the latter's historical mediation is the Christian enrolled in the present phase of salvation history (S. Brown 130).

Salvation is offered through becoming a follower of the "Way"; those followers become the community in history that proclaims Jesus' salvation to the ends of the earth.

Living As Church

United in Mind and Heart

Luke describes the early Church as a group living in unity of mind and purpose. "Now the whole group of those who believed were of one heart and soul" (Acts 4:32). Luke sees this unity, like that of the Chosen People who respond to God at the Sinai event (Deut 4:29; 6:5; 10:12; 11:13), as a characteristic of authentic believers. In fact, he speaks of unity frequently, though generally within summary statements that describe ideals for which the Church strives.

Life in the Early Church

In reality the Church struggles for unity and is often split into independent groups. There is tension among some believers in Jerusalem, Antioch, and Corinth. Nevertheless, there are efforts to build unity as an essential aspect of the faith community. The early Church makes active commitments to dialogue, minister together, share meals, foster community spirit, and offer hospitality to each other.

Hospitality epitomizes the spirit of community for which believers strive. Jesus himself is a model of hospitality in the welcome he gives to the disciples on their journey to Emmaus (Lk 24:13-35). Luke stresses the spirit of welcome that believers give to each other (Acts 15:4; 16:14-15; 21:7-14,17-25; 28:15). Converts to the faith often show this same spirit as a response to their conversion (Acts 16:34).

Missionaries cultivate a spirit of unity in the communities they establish and give the new faithful encouragement and support by helping them set up local community structures and guiding them in a deeper understanding of the faith (Acts 14:21-23). At other times missionaries call the believers together to relate all the good things God has done through their ministry, thus fostering interest and enthusiasm in their common mission (Acts 14:27-28).

According to Luke, the key to maintaining unity is a deeper understanding of the teachings of the Lord. The missionaries strengthen the community's sense of unity with other communities by sharing letters from Church leaders and instructing the faithful (Acts 15:30-33). Even after being imprisoned, the apostolic leaders' first thought upon release was to support and encourage the faithful (Acts 16:40).

Luke, aware of the struggles facing communities, still describes believers as united in mind and heart, sharing the teachings of the apostles, community, the Breaking of Bread, prayer, and material goods (Acts 2:42-47; 4:32-35). Moses anticipated such a community as a sign of God's final presence to the world (Deut 15:4), and Luke, stressing the importance of unity, shows the Christian community as a faithful expression of the eschatological community of God.

A Sharing Community

Luke's Acts gives us the most detailed presentation of Christian community of all writers of the New Testament, emphasizing the community's life of sharing. His two great summary statements on the sharing that results from faith (Acts 2:42-47; 4:32-35) stress the major forms of faith sharing: teachings, prayer, community spirit, and the Breaking of Bread. The believers' sharing witnesses to those around them (Acts 2:47), and as a result the Church becomes attractive to others (Acts 9:31). According to Luke, believers form communities that share worship, poverty, joy, and ministry.[8] Several communities add sacrificial caring for other needy members or needy communities (Acts 4:35; 11:28-29).

Luke understands that belonging to the Church and sharing the life of faith is integral to conversion. The believer's authentic expression of faith

> is not a once-and-for-all total change, but a process to be worked out *in medio ecclesiae*. The communitarian nature of Christian faith is expressed literally and radically in the lifestyle of the primitive Church (Kodell 514).

In almost every city in Acts we find the faith community gathering together to share their faith with enthusiasm and joy.

As communities become more stable and strong (Acts 16:5), they encourage each other in faithfulness to the Lord's teachings, and they also share their members as missionaries in the work of evangelization (Acts 8:14; 13:1-3; 15:22). Some readily extend their homes

Life in the Early Church

for community meetings or meals (Acts 2:46; 12:12; 16:40). Luke summarizes their life and enthusiasm: "Day by day, as they spent much time together in the temple, they broke bread at home and ate their food with glad and generous hearts, praising God and having the goodwill of all the people" (Acts 2:46).

As Paul travels to proclaim the Word, the communities gather to hear his message (Acts 15:30-33; 18:22; 21:7-14). Their affection for him is reciprocated in his constant concern for them, as when he suggests to Barnabas, "Come, let us return and visit the believers in every city where we proclaimed the word of the Lord and see how they are doing" (Acts 15:36; see also Acts 14:27-28; 15:4).

The communities' sharing in faith overflows to their willingness to share their material goods. Paul asks his communities to contribute to a collection for the needy in Jerusalem, and when he returns to the city for the last time it was to bring alms to the local Church (Acts 24:17). (Jerusalem was in need partly because of a famine but also because of their massive giving to the city's needy—a generosity that practically bankrupted their community.) Luke tells us that the Jerusalem Church "had all things in common; they would sell their possessions and goods and distribute the proceeds to all, as any had need" (Acts 2:44-45). In fact their sharing reaches the point where Luke can say, "No one claimed private ownership of any possessions, but everything they owned was held in common" (Acts 4:32). Several sell their land and houses (Acts 4:34), as does Barnabas (Acts 4:37), and bring the proceeds to the apostles, who distribute them to the community's needy. As a result of this generous sharing, "There was not a needy person among them" (Acts 4:34).

Living in Tension and Suffering

In Acts Christianity is not portrayed as having a single unified vision of life in the Lord. Several theological currents coexist—sometimes peacefully and other times not. The Jerusalem Church has two or three groups, as seen in the varied theological positions of Peter, James, and Stephen regarding the nature of the Church.

In Antioch there are signs of disunity between Jewish Christians and Gentile Christians (Acts 15:1-2; see also Gal 2:11-14).[9] In fact, there are indications of as many as four approaches to Christianity in Antioch.[10]

Stephen is martyred in Jerusalem because some Jewish leaders see him as a liberal critic of the status quo and some Christians saw him as an irritant to their desire for initial dialogue with the Jews. Stephen, "a man born before his time" (Achtemeier 25), exercises a prophetic role in the early Church. Peter is imprisoned and his life threatened in Jerusalem, and eventually he leaves the city (Acts 12:2-17). James and his followers remain but eventually cease to exist as a community. The community's demise is due partly to its very conservative approach but also to its inability to welcome the Gentiles and to break with Judaism. Our contemporary experience in and among the churches gives us insight into the pain and anguish that division and polarization cause.

The Church experiences persecution (Acts 8:1-3; 12:1-19) and faces internal divisions, too. The story of Ananias and Sapphira, who represent the disobedient Adam and Eve in the new creation of the Church, indicates the divisiveness of hypocrisy in the early community (Acts 5:1-11). We also read of the complaint of the Hellenists about the Hebrews' preferential treatment of the latter's needy widows. The clash between Paul and Barnabas and the visitors from Judea who insist on circumcision results in substantial dissension

Life in the Early Church

and debate (Acts 15:2). Paul's rejection of the young Mark, who has returned to Jerusalem because of homesickness, and the resulting conflict between Paul and Barnabas (Acts 15:37-39) give indications of the problems that exist between Church leaders.

Paul encounters opposition not only from Jews he meets during his missionary travels (Acts 13:45; 14:5; 21:27-30) but also from Christians both at the beginning (Acts 9:26-28) and at the end of his ministry (Acts 21:20-21). He even anticipates further problems after he has left: "I know that after I have gone, savage wolves will come in among you, not sparing the flock. Some even from your own group will come distorting the truth in order to entice the disciples to follow them" (Acts 20:29-30). One writer points out that Luke makes no mention of the acceptance of Paul's collection by the Jerusalem Church nor of any support given him by the Jerusalem Church after his arrest; since Luke is so concerned about showing Church unity, his silence speaks volumes regarding the tension that continues between Paul and the Jewish Christian community in Jerusalem (Pathrapankal).

Luke emphasizes unity and sharing within the context of the normal daily struggles most groups of people face. What is unique is that the Church in Acts is able to discuss its differences and search for common ground in spite of pain and anguish. Moreover, it does not seem that any of the clashes lead to bitterness or resentment; Peter and James maintain dialogue with Paul in spite of their differences. The Church grows despite its external persecutions (Acts 8:1-5; 11:19-26) and because of its mature response to internal sufferings. Luke calls for a sharing that includes communion in suffering, one that imitates the Lord's suffering and binds the group together in mutual support. In Acts we see how the Church passes through a series of crises on its way to becoming the Church willed by Christ.[11] What was said of their response to persecution can equally be said of the way they lived with tension and suffering: "they rejoiced that they were considered worthy to suffer dishonor for the sake of the name" (Acts 5:41).

A Worshiping Church

Ritual and Piety in Luke

Luke's Gospel begins with descriptions of Temple ritual and personal and community piety of devout Jews. The first two chapters are permeated with references to personal (Lk 1:47-55,68-79; 2:29-32,37), communal (Lk 2:20,41), and ritual prayer (Lk 2:13-14,22,41). Throughout the Gospel Jesus is the model of faithfulness to the piety and devotions of his day. He attends the synagogue (Lk 4:16-30), insists on ritual verification of the cure of the leper (Lk 5:14), encourages a sense of praise in recipients of his mercy (Lk 8:39), and blesses and renders thanks for food (Lk 9:16). He also cultivates a sense of devotion in others by his spirit of prayer (Lk 10:21-22), by arousing gratitude in others (Lk 10:23-24), by reminding the crowds of the providential care of God (Lk 12:22-31), and by insisting on the devotion due to the Temple of God (Lk 19:46). Jesus celebrates the Feast of Unleavened Bread with his disciples (Lk 22:8), and his own communion ritual with the disciples in Emmaus (Lk 24:30-31).

Luke deliberately ends the Gospel with the same kind of imagery he used at the beginning, but he adds an unusual twist to the account. The first story begins in the Temple with Zechariah the priest performing the rituals appropriate to Judaism. When the time comes for him to bless the people or assure them of the blessing of God, Zechariah was unable to do so because he had become dumb (Lk 1:22). For Luke, the rituals of

Judaism no longer speak to the people and no longer convey the blessings of God. The Gospel ends with a final liturgy of Christ the high priest (Lk 24:50-53), who with gestures similar to those of Simon the high priest in the book of Sirach (Sir 50:20) shows he is the one who now conveys the blessings of God. However, Jesus is not in the Temple for this final blessing—that is not where Luke now considers true mediation to be found.

In the Gospel the ascension story focuses on the glorified Lord, who returns in glory to the Father. Believers' response is that "they worshiped him" (Lk 24:52). This gesture is the basis for a new approach to worship. It marks the beginning of the new age of the Church because ritual is now focused on Jesus. Although in Acts followers of the Way still frequent the synagogues (Acts 13:14) and observe Jewish rituals (Acts 24:18), they now have a dependence on and pray to Jesus the Lord (Acts 4:23-26). They celebrate the liturgy of the Lord (Acts 13:2) and the new ritual of the Breaking of Bread (Acts 20:7).

A Community in Awe at the Wonders of God

We have already seen how Luke understands the development of salvation history to be one that unfolds according to the mysterious, predetermined plan of God. This plan is a wonderful and awe-inspiring manifestation of God's providential care of humanity. We have also seen how the early believers were constantly aware that Jesus was present to them through the Breaking of Bread, through the Holy Spirit, and through the Word. They also experienced the wonders of the Lord's power through the use of his name, a power that brought healing and forgiveness. Peter declared that the time of cosmic wonders foretold by Joel (Joel 3:1-5) had arrived with the birth of the Church at Pentecost. Later he tells the crowd that they ought not be surprised at healings in the Church; these cures are the wonderful work of the risen Lord (Acts 3:13,16). Even in times of trial, believers are in constant awe of the ever-present power of the Lord: "You stretch out your hand to heal, and signs and wonders are performed through the name of your holy servant Jesus" (Acts 4:30). We read that "many signs and wonders were done among the people through the apostles" (Acts 5:12). These signs lead to awe and hope among believers (Acts 5:15-16) and at times reverential fear (Acts 5:11).

The Church becomes accustomed to the daily involvement of God in their lives, whether through visions such as those of Peter, Philip, and Paul, through miracles worked through the apostles, or through divine protection from harm (Acts 5:19-21; 16:25-34). The signs and wonders done through the apostles become so frequent that at times non-believers end up worshiping the apostles themselves (Acts 10:25; 14:11-13).

For Luke one of the constant wonders of God is the preaching of the Word. Proclamation leads to enthusiasm and excitement in the faithful (Lk 24:32-35). This evangelization becomes so important to the disciples that "every day in the temple and at home they did not cease to teach and proclaim Jesus as the Messiah" (Acts 5:42; 8:25). The Church acknowledges God's interventions to protect the authenticity of the message, as when a vision guides Peter to begin the Gentile mission (Acts 10:9-16). When believers who initially oppose it realize God's involvement, they turn in support (Acts 11:18).

According to Luke, the early Church lives in the midst of the wonders of God and appreciates God's involvement in their lives. They learn of God's interest in them and God's desire to be alongside them in all they do.

Life in the Early Church

A Prayerful People

Luke gives special attention to the theme of prayer throughout both volumes of his work. In the Gospel he presents Jesus as a model of prayer (Lk 5:16; 10:21-22; 22:32,41-45). He prays before every major event in his ministry (Lk 3:21; 6:12; 9:18,28; 11:1; 22:41) and frequently arouses prayerful responses in his audiences (Lk 5:25-26; 7:16; 13:13). The Lukan Jesus is the teacher of prayer (Lk 6:28; 10:2; 21:36), especially during the journey to Jerusalem (Lk 11:1-13; 18:1-8).

The early Church follows Jesus' example, and Acts provides us with both communal and individual models of prayer. The Jerusalem community, gathered in the upper room, "were constantly devoting themselves to prayer" (Acts 1:14), including the discerning of the successor to Judas (Acts 1:24-25). The Jerusalem Church gives importance to prayer, going daily to the Temple to pray (Acts 2:46), praying in each other's homes (Acts 4:24-30; 12:12), and making prayer part of their community life together (Acts 2:42). In times of trial they pray for greater boldness in being faithful to the Word of the Lord (Acts 4:31) and for the release of its imprisoned leader, Peter (Acts 12:5,12). Luke also presents the community in Antioch as a model of prayer. He shows how it responds to God's call and sets aside its members for missionary work (Acts 13:2-3). In his travels, Paul often spends time with prayerful communities such as Troas (Acts 20:7-11), Ephesus (Acts 20:36), and Tyre (Acts 21:5).

Church leaders consider prayer so important that they rearrange ministries and responsibilities in order to give more time to prayer (Acts 6:4). Devoting time to prayer is one of the reasons they choose seven deacons. Peter and John go to the Temple for daily prayer (Acts 3:1), and when out of town Peter goes up on the roof of the house to pray (Acts 10:9). After Samaria hears the Word, Peter and John go there and "prayed for them that they might receive the Holy Spirit" (Acts 8:15). On that same occasion, Simon the magician tries to buy the apostles' spiritual authority and Peter tells him to pray for forgiveness (Acts 8:22). On another occasion Peter prays before working a miracle in the Lord's name (Acts 9:40) and Stephen prays at the very time of his martyrdom (Acts 7:59).

In Acts Paul's dedication to Christian prayer begins soon after his conversion (Acts 9:11) and continues throughout his life and ministry. Paul and Barnabas pray as they impose hands on elders they appointed for the communities whom they evangelized (Acts 14:23). When Paul joins with Silas, the co-workers pray regularly (Acts 16:16,25) and once try to find a quiet place by a river to pray (Acts 16:13). When Paul leaves the elders of Ephesus, they all pray together (Acts 20:36). Paul also prays in the Temple (Acts 22:17). When brought before Agrippa during his trial, Paul tells the king that he prays for his conversion (Acts 26:29). Shipwrecked and stranded on Malta, Paul prays for the cure of Publius' father (Acts 28:8).

Luke's picture of the praying Church is detailed and highlights prayers of praise, petition, thanksgiving, sorrow, and discernment. Acts is the great challenge to community prayer for Christians of every generation (Navone: *Themes* 30, "Lucan Banquet" 155).[12]

The Breaking of Bread

One of the great forms of community sharing and prayer is the Breaking of Bread. Meals play an important role in Luke's work (Lk 9:16-17; 22:14-20; 24:30-35,41-43). John Navone claims that Luke has a banquet at every significant moment both in the Gospel and in Acts (Lk 5:27-31; 9:10-17; 14; 22:15-38; 24; Acts 10:41; 16:34; 28:23). Navone suggests that the banquet theme is a "primitive ecclesiology" (Walaskay 60). In each meal the participants share friendship, conversation

Life in the Early Church

about the Lord, and learn more about their faith (Lk 24:35).

The meal of the Last Supper is not an isolated event; there are several meals in the Gospel. For example, the two disciples on the road to Emmaus recognize Jesus in the Breaking of Bread even though, seemingly, neither participated in the Last Supper. In Acts, the Breaking of Bread is an invitation to learn about the Lord and be transformed into Christ. The Word testifies to the Lord, but the Breaking of Bread brings the risen Lord to the community. Luke's approach to the Last Supper emphasizes the presence of the Lord in every celebration of the Breaking of Bread.

Some commentators suggest that the four components of early community life are really the four components of the Eucharist:

apostles' teaching — readings

fellowship — community worship

Breaking of Bread — liturgy of the Eucharist

prayers — prayers of the faithful

Others suggest that these are not four parts of the Eucharist but four distinct forms of sharing in the early Church.

This ritual becomes the focal point of the early Church (Acts 2:42), who gather to celebrate it in their homes (Acts 2:46). Luke also speaks of the Breaking of Bread in Antioch (Acts 13:2-3) and mentions that Paul celebrates it in Troas (Acts 20:7-11). During the dangers of his voyage to Rome (Acts 27:35), we find an interesting combination of events that present us with a simple theology of the Eucharist.

> Luke combines the giving of thanks to God, the breaking of bread aboard a doomed ship, and the promise of salvation to the ship's passengers....Acts 27:34-36 is, if not eucharistic, a prefiguration of the eucharist (Hultgren 363).

The Breaking of Bread is not only an eschatological banquet but the major ritual celebration of the early Church, in which believers share life, prayer, and community, and in doing so grow in awareness of who Jesus is for them individually and as a people.

A Ministering Church

Universal Call to Ministry

The Third Gospel presents Jesus' ministry as a calling to the faith that brings salvation. Luke divides his Gospel into periods of ministry: the Galilean ministry, the journey ministry, and the ministry in Jerusalem. The infancy narrative is a pre-ministry summary of the same basic theological ideas found in the periods of ministry. Acts, too, is divided into periods of ministry, following the program of action that Jesus gave in his last address (Lk 24:46-48; Acts 1:8). In Acts, Peter's ministry parallels Jesus', and Paul's parallels Peter's. In the Gospel, Jesus shares his ministry with the Twelve in Galilee, with the seventy-two during the journey, and symbolically with Simon of Cyrene in Jerusalem. Likewise, in Acts the apostles share their ministry with the deacons, Paul and Barnabas with local leaders, and Church leaders such as those in Antioch with unnamed individuals who are charged with carrying on the work of the Lord. At every level there is desire to open up the opportunities to minister to all the people, helping them to be aware of the universal call to ministry. Ministry is no longer the right or privilege of a few, selected on the basis of tribe, family, money, or political power. Rather, all members of the Church have a call to ministry.

Whenever Luke uses the term "disciple," he means disciple-minister. Luke's call to his community is a call to renewal through ministry. Acts not only shows the Church's fidelity to Jesus' command to go to the ends of the earth, but it also shows the progressive involvement of the baptized in ministry, whether they be well known (such as the Twelve), less known (such as Simeon, Lucius, and Manaen [Acts 13:1]), or unknown (such as those from Cyprus and Cyrene, who bring the message to Phoenicia, Cyprus, and Antioch [Acts 11:19-21]).

Whenever Luke speaks about ministry he refers to the same seven components. His repetition of these same seven ideas suggests that this is his theology of ministry—that is, these components are what Luke considers essential to Christian ministry for every baptized believer. He presents every minister's period of ministry as beginning with an experience in which the person becomes aware of the call to minister to others and sees that call as part of his co-responsibility in the Church. The disciple-minister always experiences rejection. The minister continues the preaching, teaching, and healing ministry of Jesus. The minister is nourished by prayer. The minister faces conflict from civil or religious authorities. Each minister, whether in the Gospel or Acts, shares his ministry with others. Finally, no minister can participate in the ministry of the Lord without participating in his cross. Luke weaves these seven theological themes throughout each period of ministry in the Gospel and Acts. He calls every believer to this type of ministry.

These common themes offer us a concrete plan for pastorally challenging all believers to participate in a contemporary renewal through ministry and to do so with the enthusiastic dedication of the model minister, Paul (Acts 20:24).

The Ministry of Leadership

Part of Luke's intention in writing is to create a sense of institutional order in the communities of early Christianity. Luke's primary focus is God's people, but he presents them as structured to facilitate their growth in the Spirit. "The Spirit mobilizes those who are receptive to its power, and the institutional is the earthly matrix in which those endowed by the Spirit act."[13] Jesus is the model of authority and leadership, consistently rejecting some kinds of authority as unsuitable for his Church (Lk 2:16; 4:6-8; 19:24-27; Pervo 41) and insisting that other kinds be fostered in his Church (Lk 9:46-50; 22:24-27).

The prime authority in the Church is the Word of Jesus. Matthew concludes his Gospel with Jesus' words: "All authority in heaven and on earth has been given to me" (Mt 28:18). But Luke writes, "These are my words that I spoke to you while I was still with you" (Lk 24:44). The authority of this Word is now entrusted to ministers, who act as the Lord's mediators and apostles (Acts 1:2; 8:35; 9:6,10). According to Acts, some were teachers, others community leaders, and others prophets (Acts 13:1).

The ministry of leadership is exercised first by the Twelve, but surprisingly they disappear from the storyline in Acts after only a short time. Since others exercise the same ministry as the Twelve, what is special about them? First, Jesus chose them; thus the Church sees them as "apostles," those specially sent by the Lord with authority (Lk 6:12-16). These people experienced a close relationship with Jesus, witnessed special events of the ministry (Acts 1:21-22), and received from Jesus the power to preach and heal (Lk 9:1-11). Luke omits anything negative about these disciples found in his source Mark (Mk 14:27,50); in Acts we see them exercising significant responsibility and leadership in the early Church, deciding critical issues as they arise (Acts 15:2). They are special because they are the foundation of the new Chosen People, the authoritative witnesses to and link with the risen Lord. They are above all important because Jesus entrusts to them the Word which brings salvation.

The Twelve exercise their authority collegially (Acts 11:1-4; 15:6,22-23) and have a sense of co- responsibility for the whole Church. Sometimes the community makes decision that the Twelve ratify (Acts 6:3-6); sometimes the Twelve make resolutions to which the community consents (Acts 15:22), and then they keep the faithful informed (Acts 15:23). In all, there are five meetings of Church leaders, each one coming "at a significant point in the community's life and growth"[14] (Acts 1:12-14; 1:15-26; 6:2-6; 11:1-18; 15:2-29). The most significant meeting is the Council of Jerusalem, held around 48-49 CE to settle the issue of Gentile entry into the Church.

Individual apostles play important roles. Peter is the recognized leader and spokesperson (Acts 1:15) and he initiates the Gentile mission (Acts 10:1-11:18). Peter is a person of authority (Acts 5:1-11; 15:7-11), a miracle worker (Acts 3:1-10; 5:14-16; 9:32-42), and a great preacher (Acts 2:14-36; 3:12-26; 10:34-43). He is also the object of special divine protection (Acts 5:17-21; 10:9-48; 12:6-11). Luke draws on several sources to portray Peter; ultimately he seems to present the Peter he thinks would have best led the early Church rather than the Peter we know from the Gospels.

Paul is the great leader of the Gentile mission, sometimes working on his own, sometimes with co-workers. Personally chosen by the Lord (Acts 9:1-19; 22:3-21; 26:9-18), he makes four great missionary journeys to proclaim the Word of the Lord. Luke often shows Paul's ministry paralleling that of Peter, thereby show-

A Ministering Church

ing that the Lord's power that was active in Peter for the Jews is equally active in Paul for the Gentiles. Paul installs presbyters in the churches he founds (Acts 14:23) but seems to retain the main authority himself. He respects Peter and James but does not imitate the structures of their churches.

James the brother of the Lord governs Jerusalem. Though not an apostle, he plays an important role in the Jerusalem Council (Acts 15:13-21), and Paul goes to pay his respects to James when he returns to Jerusalem (Acts 21:18). James may have governed a whole provincial area (Acts 15:1), much like a later metropolitan (archbishop).

In addition to Peter, Paul, and James, others exercised the ministry of leadership: the seven deacons (Acts 6:1-6), Barnabas, Silas, Timothy, prophets such as Agabus (Acts 11:27-29), local prophets and teachers such as those in Antioch (Acts 13:1-3), and elders in places such as Ephesus (Acts 20:17-35).

Variety of Ministries

The early Church gathers by the authority and challenge of the Word of God and is structured hierarchically and collegially to facilitate and manifest the call of the Word. Many individuals and groups are involved in ministry with the support of the Church. That support is institutionalized in that it came from the organized communities of the Church. In Acts ministry needs to be ecclesial even though it does not need ecclesiastical sanctioning. The Church gives the mission but not necessarily permission.

In addition to the ministers who serve the needs of internal community administration and leadership mentioned in the previous section, there is another key minister of the early Church: the missionary. Paul and Barnabas are designated by the local community to be missionaries (Acts 13:1-3) and they personally choose co-workers (Acts 15:36-41; 16:2-3). Others such as Aquila and Priscilla (Acts 18:1-4) and Apollos (Acts 18:24-28) travel around, preaching as their personal responses to their calls from God. The missionaries' primary task is to preach the Word, and in doing so they face persecution. Their trials become a springboard for further travel in the work of the Lord (Acts 8:1; 11:19; 18:2).

In addition to benefiting from leaders, teachers, and elders, several communities benefit from the charism of prophets (Acts 13:1; 11:27-29; 21:9-11). These prophets are gifted ministers who speak the Word of God to the community. They generally proclaim a challenge to be found in a community's situation, though sometimes they focus on future events.

One of the first authorized ministries in the Jerusalem Church is that of service to the needy. The apostles urge the community to select seven deacons to distribute food to those in need (Acts 6:1-2). This social service originally benefits widows but soon expands to all in need. Paul, too, organizes sacrificial giving in his communities (Acts 24:17). Besides these organized responses, several individuals feel personally called to charitable works—among them are Barnabas (Acts 4:37), Dorcas (Acts 9:36), and Cornelius (Acts 10:2).

Acts presents a series of individuals about whom we know little, except that when the Lord needs them they respond generously. Thus Ananias both heals and trains Paul (Acts 9:10-19); the mother of John Mark organizes the meetings of the local Church in her home (Acts 12:12); Judas, along with others, delivers and explains the letter from the Council of Jerusalem (Acts 15:22,32); and Lydia provides hospitality to the missionaries (Acts 16:14-16).

Luke permeates Acts with believers' awareness that they are called to prolong the Lord's ministries of teaching, preaching, and healing. The Church develops new ministries in response to its changing experi-

A Ministering Church

ences and calls forth the missionaries and people who serve the needs of the poor. The Church recognizes other ministries, such as that of prophet, when they arise.

These decades are of great interest to those of us in the Church today. Acts is a wonderful source for our deeper understanding of both what the Church was like and what the Church could be like. Luke deals with many issues still important to us—for example, the Church's role in history and the need to welcome all without discrimination.

When Luke presents the communal aspects of the Church, he presents teachings that form the basis for contemporary parish renewal. Luke calls us to live united in mind and heart, to foster a sense of sharing, and to face up to the trials and suffering that our choice of discipleship brings. He stresses the importance of ritual and piety, a sense of wonder and awe in the presence of God, prayer, and the celebration of the Eucharist. Luke presents the Church as a ministering community in which every baptized is called to continue the service of the Lord, whether in the structured forms of career ministries or in spontaneous responses to Church and world needs.

For Personal and Group Reflection

1. In places, Acts speaks negatively of the involvement of some Jews in the death of Jesus and the persecution of the early Church. While all the apostles and many other early disciples are themselves Jews, how is this negative approach to be understood today? What means can the Church today develop to foster positive relationships between Christians and Jews?

Life in the Early Church

2. Jesus preaches principally to Jews, but the Church eventually decides to reach out to Gentiles—a decision that is obviously difficult for the Church to make and causes polarization between some of the disciples. What decisions do you think the Church ought to consider making today which it has never made before?

3. The Church in Acts lives united in mind and heart. What practical decisions could you, your family, and your parish make that would deepen the sense of unity?

4. The early Church is characterized by various forms of sharing. Is this still something people want from their Church? If so, what forms of sharing do you suggest?

5. In fulfillment of Scripture, Luke points out that the Church always makes sure there are no needy people in its midst. What needs do people experience in your community? What can the Church do to address such needs?

6. Some of the great churches of early Christianity no longer exist. What do you think leads to their end? What dangers or challenges should the Church today keep in mind to assure our continuation and growth?

7. While dedicated to the unity of the Church, Paul has problems with Mark, Barnabas, and Peter. What problems do your parish teams meet in working together in ministry? What suggestions do you have to ease, remove, or manage them?

8. The New Testament books, especially Acts, present an atmosphere of awe and mystery in the wonders of God. What can you do to avoid losing this sense of mystery in your life?

9. Acts is filled with examples of personal, communal and ritual prayer. What can you learn from these examples?

10. Luke describes various forms of leadership in Acts. How would you compare them to today's form of Church leadership?

Chapter Six

Discipleship in Acts

> Repent, and be baptized every one of you in the name of Jesus Christ so that your sins may be forgiven; and you will receive the gift of the Holy Spirit (Acts 2:38).

The Gospel of Luke gives a detailed presentation of the nature of discipleship, especially in the section of the journey narrative (Lk 9:51-19:27)—a section that Luke uses as a handbook of teachings on discipleship. Acts presents the lived experience of the early Church's understanding of discipleship. If the Gospel shows us the sowing of the seed, even a tiny mustard seed, then Acts shows its remarkable growth (Lk 8:4-18; 13:18-19).[1] Moreover, as the faithful begin to move into new cultures and face new problems, we see their efforts to creatively adapt their commitment to discipleship while being faithful to the original call.

Baptized in the Name of Jesus

The Call to Discipleship

In his Gospel, Luke presents his message in two ways: in straightforward teachings and in "pictures" of the disciples. The disciples always travel in the company of Jesus and never leave his presence except to go on mission. As soon as the mission is complete, they return to his side to continue their journey with him. The relationship between Jesus and the disciples is strong, so strong that when Jesus leaves his disciples at the end of the ministry in the garden of Gethsemane, Luke describes their parting with a Greek word that means, "he tore himself away from them."

This picture of discipleship continues in Acts. We see that disciples are always in the company of the Church, never leaving the community except to go on mission. Once the mission is complete, they return to the community to share their common life of teaching, prayer, community, and Breaking of Bread. Luke's simple image of disciples is a fine presentation on the nature of discipleship. The disciples' example is a powerful teaching.

In Luke's Gospel the concept of "disciple" is much broader than in Matthew's or Mark's; "disciple" refers to every believer, both before and after the resurrection. He describes the call of disciples on twenty-seven occasions, four of them in detail (Lk 1:26-38; 5:1-11; 6:12-16 and 9:1-5; 10:1-20). Each of the detailed descriptions corresponds with one of the periods of ministry into which Luke divides his Gospel (see previous chapter for the periods of ministry).

We have seen that Luke often repeats key ideas when presenting a particular issue, thereby giving his theology of the point in question. He does this with the call scenes by presenting four common elements of an authentic call to Christian discipleship. First, every genuine call to follow Jesus comes from God and is not the result of a human preference or choice. Second, this call always demands a conversion to the person of the Lord Jesus with an awareness of one's need of forgiveness and of the power of God. Third, the call asks for a total commitment that requires detachment from anything that leads away from the Lord and a firm dedication to integrating the whole of life into one's self-dedication. Finally, every call results in a sense of mission and ministry in the believer.

In the Gospel Jesus personally calls individuals to follow him. In Acts individuals are called through the wonders and signs of God that arouse people's awe and reverential fear (Acts 2:1-13; 3:1-10; 9:3-9; 10:1-8) or through God's initiative mediated by ministers of the early Church (Acts 2:14; 3:11-12; 9:10-16; 10:9-23; 13:16). When ministers are involved in the call, as with Peter in the call of Cornelius or Philip in the call of the Ethiopian, they are aware that God's invitation precedes their ministerial efforts and that the Lord confirms their preaching with divine grace (Acts 13:48; 14:3; 16:14). Peter expresses well the conviction of all disciples: "We believe that we will be saved through the grace of the Lord Jesus" (Acts 15:11).

The call is to a personal relationship with the Lord. The invitation comes from the Lord, though sometimes through others. A response to the Lord's call and a faith commitment implies conversion, detachment, and a sense of mission.

Requirements for Discipleship

The ministry of Jesus consists of leading his disciples to believe that he knows, and is, the Way of salvation. The journey to Emmaus is an outline of Jesus' ministerial activity: he walks with those in need of guidance, listens to their story of potential despair or hope, instructs them, leads them to the discovery of truth, and enthuses them with belief that they will find salvation in him.[2]

In the Third Gospel Jesus expresses his disappointment at the lack of faith he finds in many, including his disciples (Lk 8:25; 18:8). After working miracles for people who seek healing from him, Jesus sends them on their way with a reminder that their faith has saved them (Lk 5:20; 8:48-50; 17:19; 18:42). In Acts, faith, the condition for salvation, is a gift (Acts 11:17; 15:11; 18:27) that results in individuals redirecting their lives to focus on Jesus.

For Luke "believer" means "Christian" (Acts 5:14; 6:7; 14:22; 17:34; 18:27), and the object of faith is Jesus (Acts 9:42; 11:17; 14:23; 16:31; 18:8; 20:21; 22:19; 24:24). Faith is not a commitment soon over and done with—faith is something that the believer must nourish, like the mysterious seed (Lk 8:12-15). Faith must be nourished so that it can grow (Acts 16:5), purifying the heart (Acts 15:9) and bringing forgiveness (Acts 13:39; 26:18). Faith is dynamic and constantly grows as the believer matures in relationship with the Lord. Ministers in Acts spend much of their time helping people remember who Jesus is and what he did so that they can find faith in him—a faith now lived in the community of the Church.

In the early Church, faith is linked with the presence of the Holy Spirit (Acts 2:38; 11:24; 19:2); it leads to sharing (Acts 2:44) and to the forming of community (Acts 4:32). It brings forgiveness of sin (Acts 10:43; 13:39), salvation (Acts 16:31), and the pledge of eternal life (Acts 13:48). Faith requires perseverance in trials (Acts 14:22) and acceptance of the Word (Acts 16:32).

Sometimes it seems that conversion is a result of faith; other times it seems as if conversion produces faith; still other times it seems that both ideas are interchangeable (Acts 20:21).[3] No matter which way conversion and faith are presented, commitment to Jesus includes two essential aspects: one negative (conversion) and the other positive (the life of faith). Conversion is a key theme in many New Testament writings, but Luke uses the concepts of conversion and repentance more frequently than all the rest of the writers of the New Testament combined. Jesus' entire ministry is a call to conversion (Lk 5:32; 11:32; 13:3-5), and in his final address to his disciples he passes on this responsibility to them (Lk 24:47).

We have seen how Luke frequently emphasizes the same key ideas in his presentation of a particular topic. He does this with the issue of conversion, thereby stressing what he thinks are the main components of a theology of conversion. First, conversion always requires a turning away from false values and a turning toward the Lord Jesus. It is not a decision to bind oneself to a series of laws or teachings but a personal commitment to journey through life in the company of the Lord (Acts 9:35,42; 11:21,24). Acts describes this change of life as a decision to become a follower of the Way (Acts 9:2; 18:25-26; 19:9,23). Second, conversion requires the believer to live with an awareness of the threat of personal and communal sin, linked to belief in God's merciful forgiveness (Acts 2:38; 5:31; 10:43; 13:38; 26:18). Missionaries always try to arouse in listeners' hearts an acknowledgment of responsibility for their sinful situations (Acts 2:23; 3:13-14; 4:10-11; 8:20-22; 10:43). Third, conversion requires the realization of the constant presence of the powerful and compassionate God—which, like the second component of conversion, is also a motive for conversion. Luke stresses that God is not distant; rather, believers live in the divine presence and are witnesses to God's grace in Jesus. God's presence is manifest in the miracles that testify to Jesus, in the stirrings of divine initiative in believers' hearts, which calls them to new life (Acts 2:24; 4:33; 14:3; 16:14). Fourth, conversion requires the knowledge that Jesus, the new Adam, will judge disciples on the way they have lived together as

God's people (Acts 17:30-31; 10:42-43). Jesus, the universal judge, is Lord of all and judges his followers not only as individuals but as a people.

Faith and conversion lead to a new life and result in baptism, forgiveness of sin, and membership in the Church (Acts 2:38,47; 4:4; 6:7; 9:42; 11:21-24; 13:48; 14:1,21; 17:34). Faith is confirmed by the gift of the Holy Spirit (Acts 2:38). Acts is not so much the description of individual conversions but a description of universal conversion; groups of people respond to the Word and become followers of the Way.

Followers of the Way

Journeying with the Lord

The Jewish Scriptures speak about the "way of the Lord" (Gen 18:19; Judg 2:22; 2 Kings 21:22; Isa 40:3; Jer 5:4; Ezek 18:25; 33:17; 33:20), meaning the manner in which God deals with humanity. God's way is a model for behavior, and religious leaders often challenge people to choose between two ways: the way of light, life, salvation, and God, or the way of darkness, death, sin, and perdition. God's way is best seen in the exodus and journey to the promised land, a journey in which God guides and forms the people. We learn God's way by traveling with God on the great journey of life. In the New Testament Jesus embodies God's way.

Luke often teaches through "pictures"; as was mentioned above, Luke portrays discipleship as they follow Jesus on his journeys. In the Gospel Luke reserves the word "follow" for Jesus; he finds it inappropriate that anyone else be followed. When he finds the word "follow" in his sources in reference to someone other than the Lord, he changes it (see Mk 9:38 and Lk 9:49; Mk 1:7 and Lk 3:16).

There are many journeys in the Third Gospel and Acts,[4] and they pick up both the Jewish Scriptures' emphasis on the way of the Lord (as well as the Hellenistic interest in the journeys of great heroes). Luke takes material from Mark (Mk 10:17,32), describing Jesus' final journey to his passion in Jerusalem as an exodus (Lk 9:31). Jesus' journey provides the model of authentic discipleship. This great journey (Lk 9:51-19:27), a wonderful piece of Lukan editing, is a handbook on discipleship that instructs believers on the way of the Lord and how they ought to journey through life in the company of the Jesus. The journey's emphasis is less on geography than on theology: commentators suggest it is a christological or ecclesiological or spiritual journey, meaning that as disciples travel with Jesus, they learn more about him, about the Church, and about themselves.[5]

When Peter presents Jesus to the crowds on the day of Pentecost, he declares Jesus is the person who teaches the ways of life (Acts 2:25-28). In the Gospel Jesus embodies the way of God; in Acts disciples are called to embody Jesus' way, as they engage in the great evangelizing journeys of the Church. Following Jesus on the journey of life—or better, journeying through life in the company of Jesus—becomes so crucial for understanding the nature of discipleship that Luke refers to Christians as followers of the Way (Acts 9:2; 18:25-26; 19:9,23; 22:4; 24:14,22).

The Way shows how Jesus accomplishes his redemptive mission, bringing healing, salvation, and authentic joy (see Lk 19:1-10) through his own journey of fidelity to the Father's will. He is the good Samaritan who encounters us on the journey (Lk 10:29-37). In Acts disciples like Peter, Philip, and especially Paul and his co-workers, make great journeys to preach the Way to the whole world.

Discipleship in Acts

Filled with the Holy Spirit

The progress of the Way, the Church's own exodus, is guided by the Holy Spirit (Acts 8:29; 10:19; 11:12; 13:4; 16:6-10; 20:22). Filled with the gifts of the Spirit (Acts 2:17-18), the Church sends its Spirit-filled missionaries to teach the Way of the Lord (Acts 11:23-24). Conversions are confirmed with the gift of the same prophetic Spirit (Acts 10:44; 19:6).

On the Spirit-guided Way, believers journey to an acceptance of the Gentile world. They realize that the Church's mission is to proclaim universal salvation. This journey is modeled on Jesus' vision (Lk 4:16-30), a vision that the disciples carefully observe during their "in-service training" on the journey to Jerusalem (Lk 9:51-62; 19:11-27). Jesus is in charge of the Church's journey along of the Way (Acts 23:11).

In this ecclesial phase of the Way of the Lord, the Church is immersed in the heart of the world like a seed is sown or like yeast is mixed with flour (Lk 13:18-21). Highlights of the progress of the Way include Athens, the cultural center of the world (Acts 17:16-34) and Rome, the political center of the world (Acts 28:16-31). Disciples gradually reach out to bring the Way of faith to the whole world. In Luke there is a clear link between the Way and witnessing; the disciples' witness brings about knowledge of the Way. Luke highlights the connection between discipleship and missionary activity in Jesus' journey.[6] John the Baptist understands his mission to be directly linked to the Lord's Way (Lk 3:4; Acts 13:25). Paul, the model minister, also connects discipleship and missionary activity (Acts 20:24).

Witnessing is based upon a personal relationship with the Lord. Before missionaries can teach others the Way, it is necessary that they have journeyed with the Lord (Lk 9:57-62). In the story of the disciples on the road to Emmaus in the Gospel and in the story of the

Ethiopian in Acts, neither the disciples' nor the Ethiopian's knowledge of Jesus or of Scripture is enough. They have to follow Jesus on the Way before their knowledge of him or the Scriptures comes alive for them.

The Way—God's values seen in Jesus and Jesus' vision of life seen in the disciples—challenges the world, which often follows a corrupt "way." Missionaries bring a new understanding to the world: God shows no partiality and God desires all humanity to follow Jesus' Way (Acts 10:34-35). The Church can never leave the world as it finds it; rather, it can show it a new Way.

Living in Union with the Lord

Those who wish to proclaim the Way must be filled with the Holy Spirit. This gift comes to disciples in the union they experience with Jesus in prayer (Lk 11:13). Luke sees a close connection between dedication to the Way and the minister's life of union with the Lord in prayer. In his ministry Jesus is always the model of this union with God in prayer.[7] When Jesus sends out the seventy to proclaim the Way, he instructs them on their need for prayer (Lk 10:2-13). The disciples' prayer, like Jesus' own, must be effective if the work of the Way is to progress.

In Luke's Gospel Jesus' major teachings on prayer are directed to the disciples during the journey to Jerusalem. Two special teachings about prayer are reserved for the disciples. Jesus' first teaching is a small treatise on prayer in three parts: how to pray, the need for perseverance in prayer, and confidence in prayer (Lk 11:1-13). Jesus' second teaching is also exclusively Luke's, in which he reminds the disciples to pray at all times with perseverance and insistence (Lk 18:1-8). In Acts the apostles understand the importance of prayer (Acts 6:4; 28:8). Luke's Gospel contains prayers of praise, thanksgiving, sorrow, and petition. Acts

Discipleship in Acts

stresses apostolic prayer—petition directly related to the disciples' work on behalf of the Way.[8]

Missionaries celebrate their initial success in proclaiming the Word by praying to discern the best leaders to consolidate the growth of the Way (Acts 14:23). Prayer also nourishes the disciples in their own fidelity (Acts 9:10-16; 10:9-15; 12:12; 16:13; 20:36-38), often leads them to new insights into their mission (Acts 8:24; 11:5; 13:2-3), and brings God's confirming power to their work (Acts 9:40).

In his portrayal of the journey to Jerusalem, Luke describes the disciples' union with the Lord by referring to them as "standing by" Jesus. This phrase has the same two meanings for Luke as it does for us: physical presence and moral support. The disciples persevere in their support of Jesus as later they will in their support of the Way. Peter declares to the assembly of elders and scribes, "we cannot keep from speaking about what we have seen and heard" (Acts 4:20).

The sense of identity the disciples feel with the Word and the Lord is but a reflection of the Lord's own sense of identity with his disciples. When Paul persecutes "any who belonged to the Way, men or women" (Acts 9:2), Jesus appears to Paul in a vision; "Saul, Saul, why do you persecute me?" (Acts 9:4). Paul never forgets this insight that the Church is the mystical body of Christ.

The disciples both embody the Way of the Lord and proclaim it with boldness. Jewish leaders are amazed at their courage and commitment. What starts in Galilee with the gathering of a few uneducated and weak witnesses develops into the universal expansion of the Way. The new faith progresses to Rome itself.

When the apostles seek a successor to Judas, they want someone who "accompanied us during all the time that the Lord Jesus went in and out among us" (Acts 1:21). In other words, they want someone who knows the Way because he has lived in union with the Lord as they traveled together. Later, when people witness the life and work of the disciples, they recognize that they have traveled in the company of Jesus (Acts 4:13).

Prisoners in the Spirit

Baptized in the Holy Spirit

Disciples, called by the Lord, through conversion find faith in the Way to become mediators of the Lord's power. Just before his departure, Jesus tells his disciples: "You will be baptized with the Holy Spirit not many days from now" (Acts 1:5). They are baptized "for the purpose of the Lord Jesus" and do everything "in the name of the Lord Jesus." In the Church's first sermon, Peter tells the crowd, "Repent, and be baptized every one of you in the name of Jesus Christ so that your sins may be forgiven; and you will receive the gift of the Holy Spirit" (Acts 2:38).

Baptism is the outward sign and sacrament of membership in the community of faith (Acts 2:41; 8:12). It is always accompanied by the gift of the Holy Spirit, for both go together. When the Samaritans accept baptism, the apostles send Peter and John to lay hands on them that they might receive the Holy Spirit (Acts 8:14-15). When Cornelius receives the gift of the Holy Spirit, Peter says, "Can anyone withhold the water for baptizing these people who have received the Holy Spirit just as we have?" (Acts 10:47). When explaining the events at Joppa to his companions in Jerusalem, Peter reflects on Jesus' words about baptism with the Holy Spirit and concludes that it is the constitutive component for membership in the Church (Acts 11:16-17). In one story in Acts, Aquila and his wife, Priscilla, meet Apollos and they instruct him on the relationship between faith in the Way, baptism in Jesus' name, and

Discipleship in Acts

the gift of the Holy Spirit (Acts 18:24-26). Paul meets some believers in Ephesus who acknowledge "we have not even heard that there is a Holy Spirit" (Acts 19:2). Paul proclaims the same message as the other apostles, that one becomes a disciple through faith confirmed by baptism and the gift of the Holy Spirit.

The new life the Holy Spirit brings to disciples is a life of power, similar to that in Jesus (Acts 10:38). In fact, Jesus tells his disciples, "You will receive power when the Holy Spirit has come upon you" (Acts 1:8). Disciples must not resist the presence and power of the Spirit within them (Acts 7:51-53). They are mediators of the Spirit's work of continuing the spread of the message of the Way, and so they must be sensitive to the Spirit's inspiration, direction, and challenge.

Finding Happiness in the Spirit

Christianity is not merely a dedication to teachings but a communication of the life which Jesus' Way of obedience won for humanity. Disciples who immerse themselves in this life can say with Paul that they put no value on their own lives but now live in a new way. Paul says that he is a willing prisoner of the Spirit (Acts 20:22). The disciples speak of themselves as "being sent out by the Holy Spirit" (Acts 13:4). Luke writes that "the Spirit of the Lord snatched Philip away" (Acts 8:39). Elsewhere we read that the Holy Spirit spoke to the elders in Antioch, telling them to set aside Barnabas and Saul (Acts 13:1-5), and on another occasion through the disciples in Tyre (Acts 21:4). Many of these interventions simply happen, and disciples witness them and respond to them as if they are willing prisoners to the power of the Spirit within them. Sometimes the Spirit's interventions call the Church to reassert the teachings of the Way (Acts 4:31) and at times to adapt and move in a new direction (Acts 10:19; 11:12; 16:6-7).

The fruits of life in the Spirit are confidence (Acts 4:31), the gift of tongues (Acts 2:4; 19:6), prophecy (Acts 2:17-18; 19:6), guidance (Acts 15:28), consolation (Acts 9:31), and joy (Acts 13:52). Acts tells us that the Holy Spirit gives disciples power (Acts 1:8), the courage to testify to Jesus (Acts 4:8), and the strength to denounce evil (Acts 13:9). The Spirit attests to the honesty of one's dedication (Acts 15:8), gives assurance of forgiveness (Acts 2:38), provides vocational direction (Acts 20:23), and prepares for the vision of God (Acts 7:55).

The Holy Spirit transforms the disciples' lives and enables them to strive for a fullness of life they never expected. One writer suggests that "Lucan style is characterized by...'plenitude formulas' in which is described the fullness of the Spirit" (Navone, *Themes*, 59-60). We read that the first disciples are filled with the Holy Spirit and boldness (Acts 4:31) and that deacons must be people who are filled with wisdom and the Spirit (Acts 6:3). Stephen and Barnabas are preachers who are filled with the Holy Spirit and faith (Acts 6:5; 11:24), other disciples are filled with joy and the Holy Spirit (Acts 13:52), and many believers are filled with the Holy Spirit (Acts 2:4).

We have seen that the Church is so convinced of the fullness of the Holy Spirit in its life that at times it identifies itself with the Holy Spirit. Thus, after the Council in Jerusalem the disciples introduce their resolutions by saying, "It has seemed good to the Holy Spirit and to us" (Acts 15:28; see also 5:3,32).

Perseverance in Spite of Persecution

Disciples who faithfully live the Way and proclaim its message to others find that suffering is a part of their life and ministry. Stephen is the first to die for the Lord, persecuted and condemned to death by the same groups who arranged Jesus' death; Luke models Stephen's martyrdom on the death of Jesus (Acts 7:58-

Discipleship in Acts

60). Stephen obviously knows that his address to the High Priest will not earn him any friends, yet he bluntly proclaims his faith, well aware of the opposition it will generate.

Following Stephen's death, "a severe persecution began against the Church in Jerusalem, and all except the apostles were scattered throughout the countryside of Judea and Samaria" (Acts 8:1). As part of a second wave of persecution, the apostle James, the brother of John, is killed by Herod (Acts 12:1-2). Peter and John are in constant trouble with the Jewish authorities. They are on trial more than once, imprisoned (Acts 4:3), and flogged (Acts 5:40). Paul's entire ministry bears out what God had told Ananias: "I myself will show him how much he must suffer for the sake of my name" (Acts 9:16). Some of the persecution comes from civil authorities, but most of it comes from religious authorities. The apostles speak of their anxiety at living under constant threat (Acts 4:29), and Paul speaks of his sorrow and pain resulting from the Jews' plots against him (Acts 20:19).

Persecution is an integral part of the lives of early disciples, and "they rejoiced that they were considered worthy to suffer dishonor for the sake of the name" (Acts 5:41). Luke writes that they were ready to die for Jesus' name (Acts 21:13). Jesus anticipates suffering for his followers (Lk 6:27-38; 9:23-26; 12:11-12; 14:26-27) and urges them to persevere. In Luke the only time Jesus refers to the disciples as "my friends" occurs in connection with suffering (Lk 12:4).

In Acts we learn that Jesus gives his followers an example to imitate (Acts 8:32). Jesus describes ideal disciples when he says, "You are those who have stood by me in my trials" (Lk 22:28). Though in Acts individuals suffer persecution, the real object of the persecution is the Church (Acts 8:1; 11:19), the new prophetic community that suffers as did prophets of old (Lk 6:23; 13:34; Acts 7:52).

Luke sees persecution as the work of evil people who are influenced by Satan.[9] Persecution is not a test to prove a disciple's strength of purpose but a consequence of Satan's attempt to frustrate the plan of God and block the spread of the message of the Way.

Suffering comes to disciples from sources other than persecution. Sometimes other believers unintentionally inflict suffering, and sometimes suffering derives from circumstances over which people have no control. For example, the Council of Jerusalem meets because some believers gave instructions that upset others and disturbed their peace of mind (Acts 15:24). Agabus the prophet foretells the suffering that will accompany a severe famine (Acts 11:28-29). The community in Caesarea suffers much in anticipation of the problems that Paul will face in Jerusalem, and their anxiety is painful for Paul: "What are you doing, weeping and breaking my heart?" (Acts 21:13-14). Luke writes that Paul and the community need to face their sufferings and accept the will of God (Acts 21:14).

According to Acts, from the beginning of his ministry, Paul is a person of suffering. He is mistrusted by other disciples (Acts 9:21). His travels are arduous; on his final voyage he almost loses his life. He is imprisoned (Acts 28:20), stoned (Acts 14:19), and flogged (Acts 16:22). The crowds to whom he speaks sometimes misunderstand him (Acts 14:14-15), reject his message (Acts 19:9-11), and on occasion react with fury (Acts 19:28-41). The thought of what will happen to his communities after his departure is painful to Paul (Acts 20:29-31). The Jews' rejection of his message also causes him suffering. (Acts 28:26-27). Through all this the Lord encourages Paul to endure the trials for the sake of the Gospel (Acts 18:9-11), a teaching Paul gives his communities (Acts 14:22). When Paul arrives in Jerusalem, believers show the same reluctance to have anything to do with him that they showed on his first visit (Acts 21:20-21; 9:26). After further imprisonment and neglect, Paul hears the Lord's assurance and call: "Keep up your courage! For just as you have testified for me in Jerusalem, so you must bear witness also in Rome" (Acts 23:11). When he gets to Rome after a horrifying voyage he is again imprisoned (Acts 28:16).

In Acts the Church faces constant hardship, but the good news spreads—sometimes in spite of the persecution, sometimes because of it (Acts 11:19-21). Disciples' perseverance in suffering is modeled after the Suffering Servant. Through the disciples' efforts, the small seed of faith grows. They feel impelled to live and proclaim the Way, no matter the consequences (Acts 4:19-20). Disciples of every generation need to hear the same words that motivate the early followers of the Lord: "Do not be afraid, but speak and do not be silent; for I am with you, and no one will lay a hand on you to harm you, for there are many in this city who are my people" (Acts 18:9-10).

Witnesses to All Jesus Did

Be My Witnesses

The High Priest expresses amazement at the power of the apostles' witnessing: "By what power or by what name did you do this?" (Acts 4:7). Before his ascension, Jesus commissions his disciples to bear witness to him to the ends of the earth (Lk 24:46-49; Acts 1:8). The form of solemn commissioning Luke frequently uses (nineteen times in Acts) illustrates the continuous divine guidance of the Church's mission.[10] The commission is given to all disciples because it is Luke's intent to show the Church's fidelity to the Lord's challenge. All sorts of apostolic individuals, some of them unknown individuals scattered because of persecution (Acts 8:4), respond to Jesus' commissioning.

Luke gives a series of characteristics of Christian witness. Just as it is the Church, not simply individuals, that is the focus of persecution, so too it is the community that faithfully witnesses to the Lord. The community's responsibility is to proclaim the message through some of its chosen members (Acts 13:1-3) as well as to proclaim the good news by its communal life (Acts 2:46-47). We have already seen that in every area of its missionary work the Church delegates its members to share in the ministry and to give local witness to the Lord. In Acts each period of witnessing includes assembling other witnesses to continue the mission.

The object of the Church's witness is Jesus, "all that he did both in Judea and in Jerusalem" (Acts 10:39). This good news is generally referred to as the Word of the Lord (Acts 15:35) and includes proclaiming that Jesus is the risen Lord (Acts 2:32), "Author of life" (Acts 3:15), and "judge of the living and the dead" (Acts 10:42). At one point in Acts, Jesus tells Paul what he is to do: "I have appeared to you for this purpose, to appoint you to serve and testify to the things in which you have seen me, and to those in which I will appear to you" (Acts 26:16). Therefore, the communal witnessing of the Church has a double focus: to witness by word and by life (Acts 8:25; 10:42; 18:5) to the multiple salvific interventions of the Lord in human history.

God confirms the preachers' message with a presence in signs and wonders (Acts 14:3). When witnessing, the disciples are always assured of the guiding and protective presence of God. Paul says: "To this day I have had help from God, and so I stand here, testifying to both small and great" (Acts 26:22). The power of the Word comes from God, not from the missionary (Acts 12:24). Acts is not centered on the preacher but on the Word of God, which in a mysterious way grows on its own (Acts 6:7; 12:24).

The Church gathers from time to time to interpret the message for changed circumstances. In Acts this not only includes the mission to the Gentiles but also the realization that witnessing implies justice and is embodied in social service (Acts 6:1-6). The fact that Jesus proclaims his message to the poor is an integral part of the message of the Church.

Contemporary disciples are challenged to be witnesses to the Lord and remember the criteria established by the apostles. The apostles seek people "of good standing, full of the Spirit and of wisdom" (Acts 6:3). Witnessing is communal; it takes courage; the witness' object is Jesus' work in salvation history, past, present, and future. A disciple's faithful witnessing is confirmed by God. In order that the witness' message may remain relevant, the Church, as the Council of Jerusalem did, reinterprets its message from time to time.

Witnessing in Confidence and Hope

Courage is a characteristic of Christian witness. The apostles speak out fearlessly (Acts 5:42; 14:3), convinced they can do nothing less (Acts 4:20). At times they pray for this boldness (Acts 4:31). Sometimes they show courage by leaving a rejecting city and moving on to the next (Acts 14:6-7).

Disciples sense that God is always with them in their witnessing (Acts 26:22) and this sense gives them great confidence. The Jewish leaders express amazement at the self-assurance of Peter and John (Acts 4:13). Peter expresses the basis of his manner in his first sermon: "I saw the Lord always before me, for he is at my right hand so that I will not be shaken" (Acts 2:25). Peter's first letter urges similar confidence for all disciples: "Always be ready to make your defense to anyone who demands from you an accounting for the hope that is in you" (1 Pet 3:15). When Paul and Barnabas encounter difficulties in Iconium, they do not leave; instead we read: "So they remained for a long time, speaking boldly for the Lord, who testified to the word of his grace by granting signs and wonders to be done through them" (Acts 14:3). On occasions when confidence and hope are not as strong as they could be, the disciples ask God to show divine support in the power of signs and wonders (Acts 4:29-30). On other occasions, the Lord encourages Paul to keep up his bold proclamation of the message (Acts 23:11).

Disciples with responsibilities in the community need to show courage when caring for the flock entrusted to them (Acts 20:28-31). Other disciples strengthen each other in their mission of witnessing, as Judas and Silas do for the community in Antioch (Acts 15:32) and as the Roman community does for Paul when he arrives in Rome (Acts 28:15).

The confidence and boldness of disciples helps the Church break down religious, social, and cultural boundaries and witness to the universal saving grace of God. Acts remains a wonderful challenge to all disciples. Acts invites us to face contemporary society with its often false values and to lead it to a vision of justice and compassion. Although Luke seems to present the gradual, steady progress of the Church, we need also remember his many references to hardships, trials, and strong opposition. In the face of these difficulties, it is the courageous dedication of the disciples that brings forth the remarkable spread of the good news.

Witnessing to the Lord Today

Luke has an unusual way of speaking about discipleship; he uses three techniques to emphasize the idea that discipleship is a commitment that is always realized in the present moment. He frequently uses "today" and "now." He often punctuates his narratives with a series of new beginnings that challenge the reader to remember that discipleship begins again with every new situation.[11] The new beginning, the "now," and the "today" are the moments in the contemporary believer's life.

Discipleship is a personal call of the Lord Jesus that demands a conversion to a new way of living and a dedication to faith in the Way of the Lord. Discipleship leads to a commitment to journey through life in the company of Jesus, faithful to the values he proclaims. This commitment requires sensitivity to the Holy Spirit and union with the Lord in prayer. True disciples become captivated by the Spirit, enthusiastically dedicate themselves, and persevere in their vision and dedication—no matter what persecution or suffering results. Thus they find happiness in fidelity and in a life committed to the Lord. This happiness leads to courageous witnessing to the Lord and benefits of the world.

Luke expands the concept of "disciple" beyond the Twelve to include all believers. His presentation of the universal call to holiness and ministry responds well to contemporary hopes of believers. When we consider the challenges the Church has established for itself in the last quarter century since Vatican II, Acts makes many of the same appeals. The Church today focuses on a new sense of mission on the part of the faithful, who have a sense of co-responsibility in discipleship. We see a greater emphasis on community and on parish programs that foster faith sharing. Since the Council and Paul VI, we have experienced a renewed vision of a Church whose prime mission is evangelization. Further, the Church's renewal movements stress prayer, spiritual reform, and liturgical spirituality. Perhaps more than anything, we appreciate that religion is not a segment of life, but that all life needs to be integrated in one, great self-dedication to God. We now see religion as a way of approaching the whole of life, the Way to which Christians have always been called. The Church reads Acts after celebrating the Easter mystery, reminding us that these challenges are the result of the Lord's invitation and supportive grace. Luke's call to his disciples comes to us "today" and "now," challenging us to begin again to center our lives on the Way.

For Personal and Group Reflection

1. Luke portrays disciples as always traveling with Jesus, never leaving his presence except to go on ministry. What does this say to us today?

2. Luke gives the following characteristics of discipleship: divine call, detachment, faith, conversion, and ministry. What needs to you think disciples have today that are not covered by Luke's five points?

3. Prayer is a critical component of discipleship. What roles does prayer play in your life? How do you think prayer relates to the effectiveness of your ministry?

4. The disciples are trained by Jesus during the journey to Jerusalem. In what kind of on-going training are you involved? What kind of training do you give to volunteers who work with you? How is the training Christ-centered?

5. Acts suggests that one becomes a disciple through faith confirmed by baptism and the gift of the Holy Spirit. How can discipleship be celebrated liturgically today—its origin, stages of growth, key moments of dedication?

Discipleship in Acts

6. In Acts, sometimes the Holy Spirit guides the Church to reaffirm its teachings; sometimes it guides it to adapt and move in a new direction. Give an example of a teaching that you believe ought to be reaffirmed. Give an example of a desirable move in a new direction.

7. Jesus describes his disciples as those who have stood by him in his trials. What are the trials of contemporary Christians in our society, in which there is no persecution?

8. Disciples proclaim the Word of God with boldness. Which are today's issues that Christians need to face with courage?

9. Luke urges readers to start their lives over "now," "today," with a "new beginning." Which aspects of your present life would you like to leave behind for a new start in your Christian dedication? What are the obstacles to doing this?

10. The Church reads Acts in the Easter season. What are the signs that a parish community is living as an Easter people?

Chapter Seven

Living As an Easter People

> The God of our ancestors raised up Jesus, whom you had killed by hanging him on a tree. God exalted him at his right hand as Leader and Savior that he might give repentance to Israel and forgiveness of sins. And we are witnesses to these things, and so is the Holy Spirit whom God has given to those who obey him (Acts 5:30-32).

Building Communities of Faith

Luke is an extraordinary figure in the early Church: evangelist, spiritual theologian, community leader, historian, and above all disciple. He is also an exceptional teacher, able to use content, method, and atmosphere to communicate his message. Acts tells us what he and his community think the Church should be; even within fifty years of the death of Jesus, Luke is already distinguishing between what is essential and what is culturally restricted to the time and place of the early communities.

Living As an Easter People

The early Church built up its communities of faith; reflecting on their efforts to build these communities, we see them move through five stages of group development, which contemporary group leaders still find useful. Every group moves through these five stages of development in its own historical and psychological development: kerygma, catechumenate, baptism, mystagogia, and Eucharist. These correspond to five contemporary stages of group development: convocation, human relationships, maturation of group ideal, ongoing consolidation of commitment, permanence or disappearance.

1. Convocation: Group is called together and given a reason for being together. In the early Church, this is the kerygma, the proclamation of the message about Jesus.

2. Human relationships: In this time of mutual testing, the Church sees if it believes the initiate is serious about faith, and the recipient checks to see if this life is going to be suitable for him or her. This period of mutual testing is the catechumenate.

3. Maturation of group ideal: Group accepts the ideal and commits to it. In the early Church, this is the solemn self-gift of the believer to Jesus and reception of the Lord in baptism.

4. Ongoing consolidation of the group's life commitment: Commitment is not a once-and-for-all event but is continuous, needing nurturing through further education and lived experience. The early Church referred to this as "mystagogia."

5. Permanence or disappearance: Group remains in existence to the joy and

gratitude of its members, or it divides into two new groups because of growth. Either case is reason to celebrate and be grateful. The early Church's celebration of gratitude is the Eucharist.

The three liturgical cycles of post-Easter readings use selections from Acts. They are a wonderfully combined set of readings that together form an extraordinary post-Easter catechesis or mystagogia. Parish communities develop what they wish in order to further consolidate the dedication of Easter converts, but with difficulty will they better what Luke gives us. There are nine readings from Acts in each of the three cycles. The readings of Easter Sunday, Ascension Thursday, and Pentecost Sunday are common to all three years, but the readings of the remaining six Sundays are different though they focus on similar topics. The table on the next page shows the three cycles and their readings.

Living As an Easter People

	Cycle A	Cycle B	Cycle C
Easter Sunday	Acts 10:34a, 37-43	Acts 10:34a, 37-43	Acts 10:34a, 37-43
Second Sunday of Easter	Acts 2:42-47	Acts 4:32-35	Acts 5:12-16
Third Sunday of Easter	Acts 2:14, 22-28	Acts 3:13-15, 17-19	Acts 5:27b-32, 40b-41
Fourth Sunday of Easter	Acts 2:14a, 36-41	Acts 4:8-12	Acts 13:14,43-52
Fifth Sunday of Easter	Acts 6:1-7	Acts 9:26-31	Acts 14:20b-26
Sixth Sunday of Easter	Acts 8:5-8, 14-17	Acts 10:25-26, 34-35, 44-48	Acts 15:1-2,22-29
Ascension Thursday	Acts 1:1-11	Acts 1:1-11	Acts 1:1-11
Seventh Sunday of Easter	Acts 1:12-14	Acts 1:15-17, 20a, 20c-26	Acts 7:55-60
Pentecost Sunday	Acts 2:1-11	Acts 2:1-11	Acts 2:1-11

An examination of the readings in each cycle shows a similarity of subject matter, giving a post-Easter mystagogia in nine stages:

1. Celebrating the resurrection
2. Living as community
3. Proclaiming faith in Jesus
4. Calling to repentance
5. Living faith in action

6. Evangelizing others

7. Prolonging Jesus' mission

8. Sharing responsibility and leadership

9. Bringing the Spirit to the world

According to these readings of Acts, the Church's post-Easter education of its newly baptized stresses resurrection, community, faith, repentance, action, evangelization, mission, responsibility, and the ongoing pentecosts of everyone's life.

Cycle A

Easter Sunday (ABC): Acts 10:34,37-43

Celebrating the Church's faith in the resurrection

At the end of Luke's Gospel (24:46-49) and at the beginning of Acts, Jesus commissions his apostles to wait in Jerusalem until clothed with the gifts of the Holy Spirit and then to bear witness to him to the ends of the earth. The phrase "ends of the earth" is often used by the Jews as a euphemism for the Gentiles—for example, Isaiah 5:26 and 49:1,12 (Eph 2:13; Acts 22:21). It is appropriate that our first reading of the Easter season comes from one of Peter's sermons, the one to the Gentile Cornelius. It is one of Acts' few brief summaries of the ministry of Jesus and is an excellent link between the Gospel readings of Lent and the historically rooted post-Easter faith of the early Church.

Luke stresses four issues in this reading. First, the risen Lord is the Jesus of history. Peter reminds the listeners that he is one of those who went about with Jesus in Galilee, saw him doing good, and witnessed Jesus' miraculous healings. Second, Jesus was crucified and put to death with the involvement of the Jews.

Third, Jesus rose from the dead, and Peter's proof is the appearances of Jesus. These appearances were not "spiritual," as docetic heretics suggested at the time Luke wrote Acts. These appearances were of a real person; Jesus ate and drank with the apostles. Fourth, Jesus instructed the Church to preach repentance in his name. These four elements are precisely the ones Jesus proclaimed to the disciples on the road to Emmaus and form a first brief summary of the kerygma.

Second Sunday of Easter (A): Acts 2:42-47

Living as a community, sharing all aspects of life

This reading is one of Luke's summary statements. Written in the imperfect tense in Greek, it does not describe specific events but typical things that consistently happened in the Church and which Luke considers ideal for his community. This passage is an important reminder about the key values that the community felt important to the living of their faith. The reading directly follows the account of Pentecost and shows that the major result of the coming of the Holy Spirit was not the gift of speaking in tongues but healthy community life.

Four components of community life are important to the believers: "the teaching of the apostles, fellowship, the Breaking of Bread, and prayers" (Acts 2:42). The community constantly feels the power of the risen Lord in the wonders and signs performed through the apostles. The apostles are as much witnesses as anyone else to these signs of God's power.

"Fellowship," one of the four characteristics of the community, is not as easily understood as the other three. Luke explains some of its implications: believers who share the riches of spiritual values also share their material goods so that no one is in need. While the community still goes daily to the Temple (for they still hope for the conversion of Israel), the focus of life, celebration, and worship passes to the house churches of early Christianity. Believers' faith, lived in community, impresses those who see it, and the example of this Easter people attracts others to the faith.

Third Sunday of Easter (A): Acts 2:14,22-28

Proclaiming faith in Jesus through the Church's preaching

This is Peter's first sermon in Acts, given on the day of Pentecost to a group of Jews, some of whom had family connections all over the known world. Since most sermons in Acts are written by Luke, they tend to have the same basic outline, and these sermons exemplify early Christian preaching. This sermon is no exception. It begins with a strong appeal to the audience. Once the audience's attention is secured, Peter reminds them of the well-known facts of Jesus' compassionate ministry. Miracles in particular are evidence of God's support of Jesus. Peter then tells the crowd two things: Jesus' death was part of the plan of God, and this mystery needs to be appreciated with a sense of wonder (Acts 2:17-21). However, although these events were ordained by God, many Jews in Jerusalem were guilty of participation in the death of the innocent Lord. Peter makes his audience face the facts of their own sin.

Peter urges his audience to be aware of their call, to remember, to think of sin, and to repent. He moves on to proclaim yet another motive for conversion besides awareness of sin—namely, the powerful involvement of God in raising Jesus. As in all the sermons in Acts, the preacher goes on to "prove" the teaching with the support of Scripture.

Living As an Easter People

Fourth Sunday of Easter (A): Acts 2:14,36-41

Calling to repentance with an awareness of sin

This passage is a continuation of last Sunday's reading from Peter's first sermon. All sermons in Acts climax with a challenge to conversion.

Peter solemnly proclaims Jesus as Lord. The Gentiles would understand this title as one that Caesar uses, and the Jews of the dispersion (who speak Greek) would think that "Lord" (the Greek word for "Yahweh") means God. Peter also proclaims that Jesus is Messiah, a profoundly important title for the Palestinian Jews.

Peter arouses the sorrow he seeks and urges the audience to repent and seal that repentance in baptism. This commitment to a changed life will bring forgiveness of sin and the gift of the Holy Spirit.

All the events Peter names fulfill humanity's hopes for forgiveness and salvation. Luke presents Peter as taking Joel 3:1-5 (a passage written about the daughters and sons of Israel and Mount Zion, emphasizing Jerusalem and Judaism) and modifying it so that it refers to the fulfillment of the promises of the children of Israel and the hopes of all who are far away (Gentiles).

Luke likes to conclude each section of Acts that speaks of the Church's evangelization by speaking about the success of the spread of the Word (Acts 2:41). In this passage he tells us of the large numbers of baptisms which offer proof of the power of the name and the Spirit.

Fifth Sunday of Easter (A): Acts 6:1-7

Living faith in action by responding to social need

Jesus fostered a sense of community in his disciples throughout his ministry, and they continue this commitment to community after the Lord's ascension. The

Twelve, who had been personally trained and commissioned by the Lord, take over the leadership of the early Church. They work closely with the faithful, discerning their hopes and responding to their concerns.

While the community dedicates itself to union of mind and heart, members struggle with the normal problems and growing pains of any group's development. Cultural differences between Greek- and Hebrew-speaking Jewish converts lead to pain, friction, and selfishness that threatens to divide the community. Each group begins to focus on its own people, forgetting the vision of a greater community of the Lord.

The conflict leads the Twelve to develop a new dimension of ministry, one of service to the internal social needs of the community. By doing so, they not only respond to new needs but succeed in preserving the central purpose of their own ministry to be mediators of the presence and Word of the Lord.

The community responds to the Twelve's proposal and selects seven Greek-speaking believers to serve the community's newly discerned needs. The community selects its ministers, and then Church leaders impose hands to set the seven apart for institutional ministry. These seven were referred to as "deacons," but we should not think of them in the same way as contemporary deacons because at that time the word simply referred to service; it later became a specific title for a clearly identified ministry. Although appointed to show the faith by reaching out in service to community needs, the deacons soon focus their ministry on the proclamation of the Word of God, thereby reminding us of the importance of evangelization in our own work of social service.

Living As an Easter People

Sixth Sunday of Easter (A): Acts 8:5-8,14-17

Evangelizing others and breaking cultural and religious boundaries

One of the Church's new ministers, Philip, reacts against the Jews' former antagonism to the Samaritans and preaches the Word to them, confirming its power with the power of miracles. He heals the sick as well as the divisions of centuries—both curing and welcoming a new group into the Church.

When the apostles in Jerusalem hear of Philip's successful mission, they send Peter and John to confirm the Samaritans' membership in the Church with the gift of the Holy Spirit. This Samaritan Pentecost leads Church leaders to a deeper appreciation of the nature of the Church's universal mission and also confirms the growing understanding of what leads to authentic membership in the Church—acceptance of the Word, baptism, and the gift of the Holy Spirit. This section does not propose two stages in Christian initiation or two distinct baptisms—one with water and one with the Holy Spirit. Rather, here early Church leaders are gradually understanding the essential components of Church life.

Philip realizes that no one is fully evangelized until he or she becomes an evangelizer. As Luke presents various stages in the spread of the Gospel, he ends each section, as he does this one, with a statement about the community's joy that results from the peace and confidence that faith brings.

Ascension Thursday (ABC) Acts 1:1-11

Prolonging Jesus' mission in the Church's evangelization

Luke writes about the ascension fifty-sixty years after the Lord's departure. Looking back, he explains what this event now means for his community. The ascension is the bridge between the era of Jesus' ministry and the era of the Church's mission. Luke tells us how Jesus trained and instructed his apostles, having specially chosen them to guide the Church.

The Chosen People's forty years of wandering in the desert was their most formative time. Luke tells us Jesus spent forty days teaching his apostles about the reign of God. The word "apostle" is an ecclesiastical term and indicates the early Church's conviction that these chosen disciples were "sent" by Jesus with authority to guide the Church.

Since Luke's community is struggling with the delay of the second coming, Luke presents Jesus as insisting that the apostles are not to know when the end will be. For Luke the response of authentic faith is to live ever ready for the Lord's return and, while awaiting his return, to be witnesses throughout the world. In Acts the ascension is often referred to as the ecclesiastical ascension because it urges people to get on with the work of the Church (universal evangelization) and stop looking idly up to heaven.

The ascension is not so much an ending of Jesus' ministry but the beginning of a new era in salvation history in which Jesus continues his ministry through the Church.

Seventh Sunday of Easter (A): Acts 1:12-14

Sharing responsibility and leadership; the Twelve

After Jesus' ascension the early Church spends time in prayer, awaiting the coming of the promised Spirit of God. The Twelve gather together with some women, including Mary the mother of Jesus and some of Jesus' close relatives. This first Christian community forms the leadership of the early Church. One of Jesus' "brothers"—the Greek term is a general one referring to close relatives—later becomes the leader of the Jerusalem Church (Gal 1:19). He is eventually succeeded by Simeon, also a "brother" of the Lord.

The principal leadership lies with the Twelve, who symbolically represent the twelve patriarchs or the twelve tribes of Israel. The latter were the foundation of the Chosen People and therefore the Twelve apostles are the foundation of the new Chosen People. Later, Peter will suggest a replacement for Judas so that the symbolic number twelve can be reconstituted before the formal birth of the Church at Pentecost. As the group awaits the Father's promised Spirit, they do not wait passively; they actively prepare themselves by praying for the coming of the Holy Spirit.

This short passage links together themes that are important in Luke's vision of Church: Jerusalem, the Church, the Twelve, Mary, the community, a sense of unity, and prayer.

Pentecost Sunday (ABC): Acts 2:1-11

Bringing the Spirit to the world

Luke's account of Pentecost is the fulfillment of Jesus' promise (Acts 1:8). The Holy Spirit descends on the Church on the day when Judaism welcomes its new converts. On this day the Church welcomes new members, too; this day marks the birth of the Church.

Luke's account of the descent of the Holy Spirit at Pentecost is modeled on the events of Sinai. Just as Moses ascended the mountain to receive the gift of the Law, so now Jesus, having ascended on high, receives from the Father the Spirit, which he sends as a gift, a new guide to life. This is so special an event that Luke likens it to a new creation story—the Spirit hovers over the Church as it did over the world in Genesis 1:2. He also suggests that the Spirit's descent on Jesus at his baptism is similar to the Spirit's descent on the Church.

The Spirit brings love, peace, and union. The Spirit reverses the disharmony symbolized in the confusion of many tongues at the tower of Babel; it brings the healing unity of understanding to peoples who speak different languages.

As Luke describes the crowds gathered to witness the descent of the Holy Spirit, he mentions people from all over the Mediterranean world. While they are probably all residents of Jerusalem, Luke gives readers the impression that the whole world is witnessing the birth of the Church. Thus in this story, Luke symbolizes the Church's universality, anticipates the successful spread of the Word, and teaches that the good news is not restricted to one nation or culture.

Cycle B

Easter Sunday (ABC): Acts 10:34,37-43

See Cycle A.

The Second Sunday of Easter (B): Acts 4:32-35

Living as community, taking care of the needy

Following the events of Easter and the consolidation of the faith of the early Church, the community lives together in unity of mind and heart. Luke's description of the community spirit alludes to the Chosen People's unity at the foot of Sinai (Ex 19:8) or the unity of the ideal republic Plato describes. Luke convinces his readers, whether Jews or Gentiles, that the ideals of community described in the writings of their cultures are being lived out by the early Christians.

This unity in faith overflows into a sharing of material goods, and Luke's description becomes a model for other writers in early Christianity. The Epistle of Barnabas (19) says, "Give your neighbor a share of all you have, and do not call anything your own. If you and he [or she] participate together in things that are immortal, how much more so in things that are mortal?" (See also Didache 4).

Believers hold their goods in common to be distributed according to need. Christianity is not a religion of abnegation nor does it despise the use of material goods. Christian faith leads to charity that shows itself in sharing with those in need.

The community is called together as a people, convinced of their sin and need of forgiveness. This awareness becomes a motive for conversion. However, the quality of the community's life is strengthened not only by believers' constant need for forgiveness but also by their awareness of God's continued presence and interest in their lives. Thus, the community experiences God's presence and power in the apostles' miracles—each one a further manifestation of the resurrectional power of God calling individuals to rise to a new life.

Third Sunday of Easter (B): Acts 3:13-15,17-19

Proclaiming faith in Jesus, even under opposition

By the example of their lives and the preaching of the Word, the early Church proclaims the need for faith in Jesus. When speaking of Jesus, Luke often uses several religious titles at the same time. Jesus does not fulfill only one strand of tradition but many, and each title throws light on the way others are to be understood.

In this sermon Peter speaks of Jesus as "servant" (a word which could also mean "child"), "the Holy and Just One," "Author of life," and "Messiah." He also tells the audience that Jesus fulfilled the prophecies, suffered, and rose from the dead.

These few lines contain a powerful christological synthesis that combines several titles into a visionary and challenging portrait of Jesus. The critical issue of Peter's speech is the call for his audience to rebuild their lives on Jesus. Peter acknowledges their ignorance, telling them they need to be aware of their part in the sinful condemnation of the Lord; they need to reform their lives, turn to God, and receive forgiveness.

Here as elsewhere Luke stresses that the core value of Christianity is a personal commitment to developing a relationship with Jesus. It is not so much a dedicated obedience to a list of teachings but an enthusiastic desire to know the many facets of who Jesus is and a dedication to a deeper relationship with him.

Fourth Sunday of Easter (B): Acts 4:8-12

Calling to repentance— religious leaders and institution

The fourteen sermons in Acts follow the same basic outline. Luke is the speech writer, but he seems to suggest that this outline is typical of the early Church's preaching. All the speeches climax in the call to repentance.

This reading comes from a discourse Peter gives during his first trial before the Sanhedrin. He speaks with surprising confidence, given his simple Galilean origins (a further indication that Luke is the writer). He is being tried for his cure of a crippled man. Filled with the Holy Spirit, he courageously articulates the reasons why the elders should repent and rebuild their lives on Jesus: he was sent by God, raised by God, and is the only source of salvation. He reminds the elders about a miracle worked in the name of Jesus. He insists that they were responsible for the crucifixion of the person whose power cured the man.

Having called the reluctant elders to a sense of guilt for their sinful actions, Peter uses one of the early Church's common scriptural proof texts, Psalm 118:22. Jesus is the stone rejected by the builders that becomes the foundation stone. Without Jesus they will never hold the edifice together. Peter concludes with the dramatic challenge that Jesus is the only source of salvation. His insistence on "only Christ" must have seemed shocking to the Sanhedrin, who, like religious leaders of every generation, were unable to let go of the "unchangeable truths" of their religion.

Fifth Sunday of Easter (B): Acts 9:26-31

Living faith in action in spite of persecution

The resurrection faith of the Church impels believers to action on behalf of the Lord. Paul, an energetic Jewish missionary before his conversion to Christ, becomes one of the greatest apostolic figures of the early Church.

Putting faith into action means social ministry for the seven deacons. For Paul it means speaking out fearlessly in the name of Jesus, in spite of the inevitable distrust he experiences from believers (whom he once persecuted) or the threats from Jews (who think he has betrayed them). Putting faith into action is painful for Paul throughout his ministry; according to Luke this suffering is something the Lord anticipated (Acts 9:16).

Paul's experience of the risen Lord is the great support of his life, and it must have enabled him to bear the burdens of his mission. His ministry, like that of other disciples, grows out of union with Jesus. Only those who spent time with Jesus are prepared to bring his message to others.

The reading concludes with one of Luke's summary statements. These statements punctuate Acts and tell of the spread of the Gospel. The picture is of steady, peaceful, progress under the guidance of the Holy Spirit.

Putting faith into action is a costly challenge for all disciples. For Paul, times of persecution made it very difficult to live out the implications of faith. For us, times of peace and apathy (frequently seen in our contemporary cultures) can make it even more difficult to live out our faith.

Sixth Sunday of Easter (B):
Acts 10:25-26,34-35,44-48

Evangelizing others without discrimination

Luke's purpose in his two volumes is to show the spread of the Word of God to the ends of the earth. He presents this expansion gradually, both geographically and theologically. As the Word spreads from Jerusalem to Judea, Samaria, the coastal regions, and Rome, he also shows how it is received by Jews, Samaritans, Jewish proselytes, devout Gentiles, and the whole Gentile world.

In the Third Gospel Jesus expresses appreciation for the faith of a Gentile centurion: "I tell you, not even in Israel have I found such faith" (Lk 7:9). In Acts Peter is overwhelmed by the faith of another Gentile centurion, Cornelius.

The baptism of the first Gentile is a significant event for the Church. Whether this baptism is an historical event or not, Luke clearly believes the mission to the Gentiles needs a level of authorization that can overcome the natural opposition he expects and Paul experiences—the opposition from believers who still insist on entrance into Judaism before Christianity (Acts 11:1-18). Luke presents the episode of the conversion and baptism of Cornelius and his household carefully, and he repeats it three times. First, Peter has a vision in which God instructs him to rethink the purity laws of Judaism and appreciate God's impartiality (Acts 10:9-23). This story enlists God as the source of the Church's new pastoral direction. Second, the event itself takes place (Acts 1:23-48). Third, Peter explains the event to the disciples (Acts 11:1-18). Thus, the entrance of Gentiles into the Church—a practice Paul develops—is first legitimized by Peter, the recognized leader of the early Church.

The baptism of Cornelius symbolically opens the Church to the evangelization of the Gentiles. Since Cornelius knows Judaism and is a devout individual without the "typical faults" of Gentiles (idolatry and immorality), he serves as a transition figure between Judaism and the Gentile world.

Ascension Thursday (ABC): Acts 1:1-11

See Cycle A.

Seventh Sunday of Easter (B): Acts 1:15-17,20-26

Sharing responsibility and leadership under the Lord's guidance

Luke places the episode of the election of Matthias as a replacement for the traitor, Judas, between 1:14 and 2:1. The story of the Eleven in the upper room flows naturally into the events of Pentecost. However Luke, who sees the Church as the new Chosen People, wishes to reconstitute the Twelve as the symbolic foundation of the Church *before* Pentecost—the birth of the new Chosen People. (Once Luke describes the events of Pentecost, the Church never again suggests the replacement of a departed apostle.)

Luke sees the apostles as the foundation of the Church and the appointed witnesses to the resurrection. Peter states that an apostle must be an individual who can guarantee for the Church that the risen Lord is the historical Jesus. Thus Peter recommends that the

Church choose someone who knew Jesus throughout the whole period of his public ministry and who witnessed the resurrection appearances.

All the apostles, especially Peter, know of their failures regarding the Lord. Peter reminds the assembled "brethren" (Acts 1:15) that Judas was one of the chosen Twelve who betrayed the Lord. Now the Church turns to the Lord in prayer and simple discernment to gain support in their fidelity.

The early Church always seeks the will of the Lord, whom they believe is always present to them. Although later they will develop forms of prayerful discernment to discover God's will, here we see a rather primitive form of divination: the casting of lots. By using lots, they avoid being obstacles to God's guidance of the Church.

Pentecost Sunday (ABC): Acts 2:1-11

See Cycle A.

Cycle C

Easter Sunday (ABC): Acts 10:34,37-43

See Cycle A.

Second Sunday of Easter (C): Acts 5:12-16

Living as community and attracting others to the faith

Luke understands the resurrection as the great act of God, an act that shows God's interest and involvement in human history. He presents the resurrection as a motive for faith—men and women are forced to take a stand when confronted with God's personal concern for them. The empty tomb and post-resurrection appearances of the Lord were witnessed by only a few. These few now have responsibility to inform all people of the way God's power affects their lives.

In addition to his teaching on the resurrection, Luke delves into the mystery of how God's power transforms the world. He sees miracles as prolonging or re-enacting the resurrection so that others can witness God's power that leads to new life.

Through the apostles' mediation, God continually presents the world with "mini resurrections"—the miracles. By means of these acts of God, the apostles give testimony to the resurrection (Acts 4:33). Comforted and strengthened by this support, believers gather in a well-frequented area of the Temple, Solomon's Portico, to publicly witness to their faith. This courageous witnessing contrasts with the fear of many others who nevertheless are greatly impressed by the believers' quality of life.

The resurrectional power of the miracles gradually attracts more and more to the faith. Luke says they "were added" (Acts 5:14) to the Church. The passive tense here indicates that God is the source of this growth. The extraordinary power of God in the community is greater than anything Luke knows of. He describes the people carrying their sick into the streets so that Peter's shadow will fall on them and heal them. All these extraordinary healings bear witness to the resurrection.

Third Sunday of Easter (C): Acts 5:27-32,40-41

Proclaiming faith in Jesus—
the Church's inescapable obligation

In Luke's Gospel Jesus tells his disciples, "You will be brought before kings and governors because of my name. This will give you an opportunity to testify" (Lk

21:12-13). Following their many miracles, the High Priest imprisons the apostles (Acts 5:17-18), but the Lord delivers them.

This reading marks the second apprehension. The apostles are brought before the Sanhedrin. Peter speaks up, establishing the guiding principle for all authentic religion—the pursuit of God's will. For decades Peter had believed God's will was discovered primarily through the guidance of the religious leaders of his nation. Like devout believers of every generation, he needs to accept responsibility for his decisions and life. While respecting religious leaders, he cannot hide behind a belief that these leaders are always right. They had put Jesus to death to preserve the status quo, and Peter denounces their infidelity and failure to give authentic leadership.

Peter then proclaims the genuine values of religion that the so-called leaders had failed to see: Jesus is Lord, Savior, and the only source of forgiveness. Peter courageously witnesses to this in obedient response to the Holy Spirit. The Sanhedrin, the most respected religious leaders in the nation, order the apostles not to speak about Jesus and these new teachings that are so disturbing to them. The apostles know that to witness to Jesus is their inescapable obligation, and they rejoice that they are faithful in spite of ill-treatment.

Fourth Sunday of Easter (C): Acts 13:14,43-52

Calling to repentance—all peoples of the world

Jesus addresses his inaugural sermon in Nazareth to the Jews but ends by telling them he would go to the Gentiles (Lk 4:16-30). Peter does the same at Pentecost (Acts 2:14-36). While we know Paul preaches in Damascus (Acts 9:20), Jerusalem (Acts 9:28-29), Antioch (Acts 11:25-26), and most likely in Caesarea and Tarsus (Acts 9:30), his first recorded sermon is in Pisidian Antioch where he, too, speaks to the Jews but ends by telling them he will go to the Gentiles.

In this reading Paul and his co-worker Barnabas meet many converts to Judaism, urging them to hold fast to their commitment to seek God's will and grace. Later the disciples' proclamation of the Word is met with violent and abusive rejection. Paul points out that rejecting the Word's challenge to repentance and new life amounts to the rejection of eternal life.

Luke says that those who "had been destined for eternal life became believers" (Acts 13:48). This does not imply a denial of personal freedom and responsibility but refers to the conviction that all that happens is part of the sovereign will of God. The passive tense indicates God is the subject, gracing all with the same call and permitting and respecting everyone's freedom to accept or reject.

The call to change one's way of life is a joyful and liberating invitation for some. For others it implies letting go of past values, which they feel implies abandonment and failure, and they fight against such change.

Fifth Sunday of Easter (C): Acts 14:21-27

Living faith in action
through the energetic work of missionaries

The early Church witnesses to its faith in organized social service and spontaneous works of charity. But according to Acts, its prime manifestation of faith in action is the dedicated self-gift of missionaries, who relentlessly work for the spread of the Word.

This reading describes the first of Paul's four great missionary journeys. Accompanied by Barnabas, the missionaries are ill-treated in Antioch, Iconium, and Lystra but, after preaching in Derbe, they return to the cities in which they had been persecuted. When they preach the need to accept suffering, they are willing to live the response they urge on others. They do not avoid places of persecution but dedicate themselves to establishing the faith at all costs. In each town they organize local communities, installing elders to maintain the communities' faith.

The apostles' journey is long and traveling is dangerous, but they are not content to stay home in comfort and security. Their dedication to Christ and his Word leads them to reach out to others, showing their faith in action.

When they return to the Antiochean Church that missioned them in the first place (Acts 13:1-3), they share all the wonderful things that have happened in their ministry. As elsewhere in Acts, Luke reminds us that the source of all the transforming effects of ministry is not the missionary (Lk 17:10) but rather God, who works through the mediation of the Church.

Sixth Sunday of Easter (C): Acts 15:1-2,22-29

Evangelizing others without burdening them

The community in Antioch has several strong subgroups, each with its own idea of what constitutes the essence of membership in the Church. One group views the Church as part of Judaism and requires fidelity to the Mosaic Law as part of Christianity. Some believers in Jerusalem hold similar views and send visitors to Antioch to reinforce this position (see Gal 2:11-14). Paul and Barnabas respond to the Lord's call to go to the Gentiles (Acts 13:46) and understand that Christian faith implies an independent identity from Judaism. The disagreement between the apostles and the Judean visitors becomes so heated that they decide to go to Jerusalem to discuss the matter with the apostles and elders.

All the apostles gather together for the Council of Jerusalem around 48-49 CE. In verses that are not part of this reading (Acts 15:7-11), Peter reminds the apostles and elders of his vision and the resulting baptism of the Gentile Cornelius. Peter reminds the leaders that acceptance of the Gentiles is ordained by God. James, the leader of the more conservative Jerusalem Church, summarized the unanimous position of the Church leaders and suggests their views be drafted in a letter and communicated by four of the leaders. The Church decides—and believes their discerned discussion is a form of guidance from the Holy Spirit (Acts 15:28)—that no restrictions be imposed on Gentiles.

Foreigners resident in Palestine need to respect four national requirements (Acts 15:29), and the Church agrees these should stay in effect. The whole Church decides that no further requirements be imposed. They signify their desire to welcome all with the salvific grace of the Word of God.

Ascension Thursday (ABC): Acts 1:1-11

See Cycle A.

Seventh Sunday of Easter (C): Acts 7:55-60

Sharing responsibility and leadership through martyrdom

Luke presents Jesus as the protomartyr of Christianity and models Stephen's death on Jesus'. "Martyr" means "witness" and refers to the courageous confessing of Jesus even when that testimony leads to death.

Stephen is filled with the Holy Spirit and preaches even to those he anticipates can harm him. His sermon before the High Priest climaxes with his confession of Jesus as the "Son of Man" (Acts 7:56), a term that signifies final judge of the world (Dan 7:13-14).

Acts mentions the leadership of the Twelve, of Paul, and of many missionaries and local elders. The early Church also recognizes leadership in faith proclaimed by the martyr, establishing many privileges for those who confess their faith through persecution. Some show leadership in the Word they proclaim, others in the life they live, and still others in the death they endure for the name.

Stephen's death is modeled on Jesus'—even to the point of asking forgiveness for those who put him to death (Acts 7:60; Lk 23:34). As he dies he has a vision of the Son of Man standing beside the Father's throne (Acts 7:56). Jesus' posture indicates a sense of urgency, as if the end is now going to begin. Stephen bluntly challenges people to face the fact that with Jesus there is a radical break and a new beginning.

There is no place for compromise; Stephen calls all religious leaders to never oppose the challenge of the Holy Spirit but instead to always be open to the newness of life that God brings.

Pentecost Sunday (ABC): Acts 2:1-11

See Cycle A.

Afterword

In this book, we have studied what kind of author Luke is. Historian of the ancient world, he gives us a vision of both Christian origins and of contemporary challenges to our faith today. Luke is an outstanding historian, provided we judge him by the standards of his day and not ours. He describes with enthusiasm the early Church's growth and expansion. He also challenges us to build our communities of faith as early believers did. He is a great theologian and pastoral leader, and his proclamation of the Word has perennial value.

Luke is a theologian who gives us a vision of the Church dedicated to universal salvation through a ministry of evangelization. All his efforts center on the Word: listening to it, sharing it, proclaiming it, and interpreting it.

Luke is a wonderful spiritual guide who shows believers how God bursts into life every day: ever-present to humanity as merciful Father, Living Lord, and Guiding Spirit. God, who is Sovereign Lord, is also close to us and involved and interested in our history.

Afterword

Luke is a visionary of early Christianity. He gives us an understanding of Church life that is unavailable from any other New Testament writer. He enthusiastically addresses the Church's mission to bring all the world to Christ. He challenges the Church in its outreach to others and in the quality of its internal life of union, sharing, worship, prayer, and ministry.

Luke is a dedicated disciple, committed to following the Way, going nowhere except in the company of the Lord. He urges us to live in union with the Lord and to find happiness in the Spirit. He lived as a witness to all Jesus did and urges constant confidence and hope, even in the midst of persecution.

Luke is a great catechist who teaches us how to live as an Easter People. He describes the first Easter and the community it gave birth to, but he also reminds us that "today" and "now" provide an opportunity for a new beginning for each of us.

Acts of Apostles describes the great deeds of the early Church's apostolic heroes. It is a model and challenge for today's apostolic heroes, too, so that their great deeds will help bring God's transforming Word to the ends of the earth.

Notes

Introduction

1. See Cobb 185-186: "The Eastertide lections were probably the first to be fixed; Acts seems to have been read in both East and West (Augustine, *Serm.* 6 on St. John; John Chrysostom, *Serm.* 1 on Acts, *Cur in Pentecoste Acta legantur*, PG 60.22)...."

Chapter One

1. See Irenaeus in his treatise *Against Heresies* III, I, written about 178; *The Muratorian Canon* of authoritative books of Scripture, written in Rome about 180-200; the so-called *Anti-Marcionite Prologue*, dated around 180; Clement of Alexandria in *Stromateis*, V, 12 (c. 208-211); Tertullian in his *Adversus Marcionem*, IV, 2 (c. 207-208); Origen as quoted by Eusebius, and Eusebius himself in his *Historia Ecclesiastica*, III, 4, 24 (c. 311-325); and later Jerome in *De Viris Illustribus*, VIII (c. 392).

2. For additional biographical information on Luke, gleaned from the early writings, see Kelly 113-119 and Glover 97-106.

3. One of several exceptions to this position is found in Franklin 75-79, where he speaks of the influence of the Jewish Scriptures and the Jewish faith on Luke.

Notes

4. See the detailed analysis in L. Doohan, *Luke*, 13-17. For additional details on the two portraits, see Haenchen 112-116, Goodenough 51-59, and Vielhauer 33-50.

5. A growing number of writers disregard the differences as secondary, claiming that such differences offer no surprise in other ancient documents and that the importance of the differences is largely due to modern interpreters. These writers believe there is substantial agreement between the two portraits and that the Paul of Acts is a retrospective portrait of a friend, namely Luke. See Bruce, "Is the Paul of Acts the Real Paul?" 282-305; Borgen 169-182; Hultgren 353-365.

6. See Pervo 145: "Paul was there [in the letters] accused of insufficient miracles, lack of power and prestige, poor speaking ability, and failure to have adequate credentials, including letters of recommendation. Acts attributes just these qualities to Paul."

7. Some writers, acknowledging the differences, suggest that they can be reconciled if one sees Acts as an idealization of Paul by Luke, who had a short association with him but not during the major crises or maturing points of Paul's life and ministry. See Fitzmyer 28 and L. Doohan, *Luke*, 16-17.

8. See L. Doohan, *Luke*, chapter 2.

9. Bruce (*Acts* 23) is not impressed with these double episodes: "...these pairs are not simply doublets, and the narrative...reads smoothly and continuously without having recourse to source-analysis."

10. See L. Doohan, *Luke*, chapter 2.

11. See Talbert, Wolfe, and Robbins.

12. See Parker; Marshall, "Recent Study"; Munck xlviii; Bruce, *Acts*, 11-13; Mattill, "Date and Purpose."

13. See O'Neill, *Theology*, 1-58; Knox; Wilshire.

14. The only way commentators can hold an early date of Acts while accepting the Third Gospel's dependence on Mark is to suggest that Acts predates Mark but the Third Gospel comes after Mark. This means that when Luke refers to his first volume (Acts 1:1), it can only be a prior lost

manuscript. But hypothesis based on hypothesis has never received much support.

15. For more about form criticism, see L. Doohan, *Luke*, 163-164.

16. For articles that analyze recent developments in Luke-Acts, see Gasque; Harrington; Marshall, "Present State"; Powell, "Are the Sands Still Shifting?"

Chapter Two

1. See Brown and Meier, Introduction.

2. For further discussion about the Church's relationship with the empire, see chapter 3, pages 76-78.

Chapter Three

1. For further study of the styles of the evangelists, see L. Doohan: *Mark* 16-19; *Matthew* 17-20; *John* 41-46.

2. See Fenton.

3. For the six common themes, see Kee, Young, and Froehlich 393: Jesus is of Davidic ancestry, his ministry was approved by God, his death at the hands of the Jews fulfilled Scripture, now the Gentiles ought to recognize God's concern for them, God approved Jesus' life and ministry by raising him from the dead and sending the Holy Spirit, and all men and women are called to repentance and to receive salvation in Jesus. For the common outline of the speeches, see Schweizer.

4. Bruce, *Acts*, 18 quotes the classical historian Thucydides (1. 22), who refers to several speeches in his own work: "I have recorded them in accordance with my opinion of what the various speakers would have had to say in view of the circumstances at the time, keeping as closely as possible to the general history of what was really said."

5. Marshall, *Luke*, 73 expresses an opposing view: "In short, it is one-sided to look at the speeches in Acts merely as evidence for Luke's theology, they have a claim to be based on the practice of the early Church."

Notes

6. See Ladouceur.

7. See Marshall, *Luke*, especially chapter 8.

8. See Dupont.

9. See Pervo 138: "Appealing to all that was progressive and idealistic in the church's structures, Luke offered, so to speak, its services to the imperial society of his day. Christianity, which Luke viewed as a renewed form of Judaism stripped of its limitations, had both the interest in and the means for elevating the rude and unwashed masses, for promoting urbanity and ethics, community and loyalty."

10. See Goodenough 58.

11. There are five trial scenes involving Paul. See Trites.

12. See also Cadbury 316; Danker 104.

13. See L. Doohan, *Luke*, chapter 3.

14. See Grumm.

Chapter Four

1. See Moule; J. A. T. Robinson.

2. See L. Doohan, *Luke*, 71-80.

3. Some writers accuse Luke of subordinationism and adoptionism. See Wilckens 62; Conzelmann 174; Drury 123.

4. See Moule.

5. See Owen.

6. See O'Toole.

7. See Stravinskas.

8. See Navone, *Themes*, 158.

Chapter Five

1. See L. Doohan, *Luke*, 88-90.

2. See L. Doohan, *Luke*, 145-149.

3. See Tyson.

Notes

4. See Drury 183.

5. See L. Doohan, *Luke*, 166-171; Elliot; Hultgren.

6. For general syntheses of Luke's eschatology, see Mattill, *Luke*; Kurz; Malina.

7. See Wilson.

8. See L. Doohan, *Luke*, 103-108.

9. See Achtemeier 11.

10. See R. Brown.

11. For additional material on prayer in Luke-Acts, see H. and L. Doohan 60-65, 86-94.

12. See also Smith 638.

13. See Powell, "Religious Leaders."

14. For more detailed descriptions of the authority structures in the early Church and some of its significant leaders, see L. Doohan, *Luke*, 98-103.

Chapter Six

1. See Juel 87.

2. See D'Arc.

3. See S. Brown 90; Marshall, *Luke*, 194; Conzelmann 219.

4. See L. Doohan, *Luke*, 116-119.

5. See L. Doohan, *Luke*, 118-119.

6. See Gill 204-205.

7. See Edmonds.

8. See H. and L. Doohan 60-65.

9. See S. Brown 130.

10. See Hubbard: "Commissioning Stories in Luke-Acts"; "Role of the Commissioning Accounts in Acts."

11. See L. Doohan, *Luke*, 128-130.

Resources

Achtemeier, Paul J. "An Elusive Unity: Paul, Acts, and the Early Church." *Catholic Biblical Quarterly* 48 (1986): 1-26.

Betz, Otto. "The Kerygma of Luke." *Interpretation* 12 (1968): 131-146.

Borgen, Peder. "From Paul to Luke." *Catholic Biblical Quarterly* 31 (1969): 169-182.

Brown, Raymond E., and John P. Meier. *Antioch and Rome*. New York: Paulist Press, 1982.

Brown, Raymond E. "Not Jewish Christianity and Gentile Christianity but Types of Jewish/Gentile Christianity." *Catholic Biblical Quarterly* 45 (1983): 74-79.

Brown, Schuyler. *Apostasy and Perseverance in the Theology of Luke*. Rome: Pontifical Biblical Institute, 1969.

Bruce, F. F. *The Acts of the Apostles*. Grand Rapids, Michigan: William B. Eerdmans Publishing Co., 1951.

———. "The Holy Spirit in Acts of Apostles." *Interpretation* 27 (1973): 166-183.

———. "Is the Paul of Acts the Real Paul?" *Bulletin of John Ryland's University Library* 58 (1976): 282-305.

Cadbury, H. J. *The Making of Luke-Acts*. London: SPCK, 1968.

Resources

Caird, G. B. *St. Luke*. Harmondsworth: Penguin Books, 1963.

Cassidy, Richard, and Philip Scharper, eds. *Political Issues in Luke-Acts*. Maryknoll, NY: Orbis Books, 1983.

Cobb, Peter G. "The Liturgy of the Word in the Early Church." In *The Study of Liturgy*, edited by Cheslyn Jones, Geoffrey Wainwright, and Edward Yarnold, 185-186. New York: Oxford University Press, 1978.

Conzelmann, Hans. *The Theology of St. Luke*. New York: Harper and Row, 1960.

D'Arc, J. "Catechesis on the Road to Emmaus." *Lumen Vitae* 32 (1977): 143-156.

Danker, F. *Luke: Proclamation Commentaries*. Philadelphia: Fortress Press, 1976.

Doohan, Helen. *Paul's Vision of Church*. Collegeville, MN: Liturgical Press/Michael Glazier Books, 1989.

Doohan, Helen and Leonard. *Prayer in the New Testament*. Collegeville, Minnesota: Liturgical Press, 1992.

Doohan, Leonard. *John: Gospel for a New Age*. Santa Fe: Bear and Company, 1988. Write to Resource Publications, 160 East Virginia Street #290, San Jose, CA 95112.

———. *Luke: The Perennial Spirituality*. Santa Fe: Bear and Company, 1985. Write to Resource Publications, 160 East Virginia Street #290, San Jose, CA 95112.

———. *Mark: Visionary of Early Christianity*. Santa Fe: Bear and Company, 1986. Write to Resource Publications, 160 East Virginia Street #290, San Jose, CA 95112.

———. *Matthew: Spirituality for the 80s and 90s*. Santa Fe: Bear and Company, 1985. Write to Resource Publications, 160 East Virginia Street #290, San Jose, CA 95112.

Drury, John. *Tradition and Design in Luke's Gospel*. Atlanta: John Knox Press, 1977.

Dupont, Jacques. *The Salvation of the Gentiles*. New York: Paulist Press, 1979.

Edmonds, P. "The Lucan Our Father: A Summary of Luke's Teachings on Prayer?" *Expository Times* 91 (1980): 140-143.

Elliot, John H. "A Catholic Gospel: Reflections on 'Early Catholicism' in the New Testament." *Catholic Biblical Quarterly* 31 (1969): 213-223.

Fenton, J. "The Order of the Miracles Performed by Peter and Paul in Acts." *Expository Times* 77 (1966): 381-383.

Fitzmyer, Joseph A. *The Gospel According to Luke.* New York: Doubleday and Co., Inc., 1981.

Franklin, Eric. *Christ the Lord: A Study in the Purpose and Theology of Luke-Acts.* Philadelphia: Westminster Press, 1975.

Gasque, W. W. "Recent Commentaries on the Acts of the Apostles." *Themelios* 14 (1988): 21-23.

Gill, D. "Observations on the Lukan Travel Narrative and Some Related Passages." *Harvard Theological Review* 63 (1970): 199-221.

Glover, Richard. "'Luke the Antiochene' and Acts." *New Testament Studies* 11 (1964): 97-106.

Goodenough, Edwin R. "The Perspective of Acts." In *Studies in Luke-Acts,* edited by L. E. Keck and J. L. Martyn, 51-59. New York: Abingdon Press, 1966.

Grumm, M. H. "Another Look at Acts." *Expository Times* 96 (1985): 333-337.

Haenchen, Ernst. *The Acts of the Apostles.* Oxford: Blackwell, 1971.

Harrington, Wilfrid. "New Testament Theology: Two Recent Approaches." *Biblical Theology Bulletin* 1 (1971): 171-189.

Hengel, Martin. *Acts and the History of Earliest Christianity.* Philadelphia: Fortress Press, 1980.

Hubbard, Benjamin. "Commissioning Stories in Luke-Acts: A Study of the Antecedents, Form and Content." *Semeia* 8 (1977): 107-126.

Resources

———. "The Role of the Commissioning Accounts in Acts." In *Perspectives on Luke-Acts,* edited by C. H. Talbert, 187-198. Danville, Virginia: Association of Baptist Professors of Religion, 1978.

Hultgren, Arland. "Interpreting the Gospel of Luke." *Interpretation* 30 (1976): 353-365.

Juel, Donald. *Luke-Acts: The Promise of History.* Atlanta: John Knox Press, 1983.

Keck, L. E., and J. L. Martyn, eds. *Studies in Luke-Acts.* New York: Abingdon Press, 1966.

Kee, H. C., F. W. Young, and K. Froelich. *Understanding the New Testament.* 3rd. ed. Englewood Cliffs, New Jersey: Prentice Hall, Inc., 1973.

Kelly, Joseph. "The Patristic Biography of Luke." *Bible Today* 74 (1974): 113-119.

Knox, J. "Acts and the Pauline Letter Corpus." In *Studies in Luke-Acts,* edited by L. E. Keck and J. L. Martyn, 302-304. New York: Abingdon Press, 1966.

Kodell, Jerome. "'The Word of God Grew.' The Ecclesial Tendency of Logos in Acts 1:7; 12:24; 19:20." *Biblica* 55 (1974): 505-519.

Kurz, William S. "Response to the End of History: Eschatology and Situation in Luke-Acts." *Catholic Biblical Quarterly* 51 (1989): 553-554.

Ladouceur, D. "Hellenistic Preconceptions of Shipwreck and Pollution as a Context for Acts 27-28." *Harvard Theological Review* 73 (1980): 435-449.

Lampe, G. W. H. "The Lucan Portrait of Christ." *New Testament Studies* 2 (1955-56): 160-175.

Leaney, A. R. C. *The Gospel According to St. Luke.* London: Adam and Charles Black, 1974.

MacRae, George. "'Whom Heaven Must Receive Until the Time': Reflections on the Christology of Acts." *Interpretations* 27 (1973): 151-165.

Malina, Bruce J. "Christ and Time: Swiss or Mediterranean?" *Catholic Biblical Quarterly* 51 (1989): 1-31.

Marshall, I. Howard. "Recent Study of the Acts of the Apostles." *Expository Times* 80 (1969): 292-296.

———. *Luke: Historian and Theologian*. Grand Rapids, Michigan: Zondervan, 1971.

———. "The Present State of Lucan Studies." *Themelios* 14 (1989): 47-52.

Mattil, A. J. Jr. "The Date and Purpose of Luke-Acts: Rackham Reconsidered." *Catholic Biblical Quarterly* 40 (1978): 335-350.

———. *Luke and the Last Things*. Dillsboro, North Carolina: Western North Carolina Press, 1979.

Minear, Paul S. "Dear Theo, The Kerygmatic Intention and Claim of the Book of Acts." *Interpretation* 27 (1973): 131-150.

Moule, C. F. D. "The Christology of Acts." In *Studies in Luke-Acts*, edited by L. E. Keck and J. L. Martyn, 159-185. New York: Abingdon Press, 1966.

Munck, Johannes. *The Acts of the Apostles*. New York: Doubleday and Co., Inc., 1967.

Navone, John. *Themes of St. Luke*. Rome: Gregorian University Press, 1970.

———. "The Lucan Banquet Community." *Bible Today* 8 (1970): 155-161.

O'Neill, J. C. "The Six Amen Sayings in Luke." *Journal of Theological Studies* 10 (1959): 1-9.

———. *The Theology of Acts in Its Historical Setting*. London: SPCK, 1961.

O'Toole, R. F. "Activity of the Risen Jesus in Luke-Acts." *Biblica* 62 (1981): 471-498.

Owen, H. P. "Stephen's Vision in Acts VII:55-56." *New Testament Studies* 1 (1955-56): 224-225.

Resources

Parker, Pierson. "The 'Former Treatise' and the Date of Luke-Acts." *Journal of Biblical Literature* 86 (1967): 175-182.

Pathrapankal, J. "Creative Crises of Leadership in the Acts of the Apostles." *Indian Journal of Theology* (1985): 52-60.

Pervo, Richard I. *Profit with Delight: The Literary Genre of the Acts of the Apostles.* Philadelphia: Fortress Press, 1987.

Powell, Mark Allan. "Are the Sands Still Shifting? An Update on Lukan Scholarship." *Trinity Seminary Review* 11 (1989): 15-22.

———. "The Religious Leaders in Luke: A Literary-Critical Study." *Journal of Biblical Literature* 109 (1990): 95-109.

Praeder, Susan Marie. "Acts 27:1-28:16: Sea Voyages in Ancient Literature and the Theology of Luke-Acts." *Catholic Biblical Quarterly* 46 (1984): 683-706.

Robbins, Vernon K. "Prefaces in Greco-Roman Biography and Luke-Acts." *Perspectives in Religious Studies* 6 (1979): 94-108.

Robinson, J. A. T. "The Most Primitive Christianity of All." *Journal of Theological Studies* 7 (1956): 177-189.

Robinson, William C. "On Preaching the Word of God (Luke 8:4-21)." In *Studies in Luke-Acts*, edited by L. E. Keck and J. L. Martyn, 131-138. New York: Abingdon Press, 1966.

Schweizer, E. "Concerning Speeches in Acts." In *Studies in Luke-Acts*, edited by L. E. Keck and J. L. Martyn, 210-212. New York: Abingdon Press, 1966.

Simon, Richard. *A critical history of the text of the New Testament.* London, 1689.

Smith, Dennis E. "Table Fellowship as a Literary Motif in the Gospel of Luke." *Journal of Biblical Literature* 106 (1987): 613-638.

Stravinskas, P. "The Role of the Spirit in Acts 1 and 2." *Bible Today* 18 (1980): 263-268.

Talbert, Charles H. *Literary Patterns, Theological Themes and the Genre of Luke-Acts.* Missoula, Montana: Scholars' Press, 1974.

Trites, A. A. "The Importance of Legal Scenes and Language in the Book of Acts." *Novum Testamentum* 16 (1974): 278-284.

Tyson, J. B. "The Gentile Mission and the Authority of Scripture in Acts." *New Testament Studies* 33 (1987): 619-631.

van Stempvoort, P. A. "The Interpretation of the Ascension in Luke and Acts." *New Testament Studies* 5 (1958-59): 30-42.

van Unnik, W. C. "Luke-Acts, A Storm Center in Contemporary Scholarship." In *Studies in Luke-Acts*, edited by L. E. Keck and J. L. Martyn, 15-32. New York: Abingdon Press, 1966.

Vielhauer, Paul. "On the Paulinism of Acts." In *Studies in Luke-Acts*, edited by L. E. Keck and J. L. Martyn, 33-50. New York: Abingdon Press, 1966.

Walaskay, Paul. *"And So We Came To Rome": The Political Perspective of St. Luke*. New York: Cambridge University Press, 1983.

Wilckens, Ulrich. "Interpreting Luke-Acts in a Period of Existentialist Theology." In *Studies in Luke-Acts*, edited by L. E. Keck and J. L. Martyn, 60-83. New York: Abingdon Press, 1966.

Wilshire, L. E. "Was Canonical Luke Written in the Second Century? A Continuing Discussion." *New Testament Studies* 20 (1974): 246-253.

Wilson, S. G. "Lukan Eschatology." *New Testament Studies* 16 (1970): 330-347.

Wolfe, K. R. "The Chiastic Structure of Luke-Acts and Some Implications for Worship." *SW Journal of Theology* 22 (1980): 60-71.

Index of Scripture References

Genesis	
1:2	172
18:19	144

Exodus	
19:8	173
25:22	34

Numbers	
11:24-30	34

Deuteronomy	
4:29	117
6:5	117
10:12	117
11:13	117
12:2-5	34
15:4	119
18:15	98

Judges	
2:22	144

1 Kings	
6:37-38	34

2 Kings	
2:7-13	34
2:10	102
21:22	144

1 Chronicles	
28:3-7	34

Psalms	
118:22	176

Sirach	
50:20	124

Isaiah	
2:1-5	35
2:2-4	35
5:26	165
6:1-3	35
40:3	144
40:9-11	35
42:1-7	96
44:3-5	102
49:1,12	165
49:1-7	96
50:4-9	96
52:13-53:12	96

Scripture References

Jeremiah		1:69	98
5:4	144	2	94
7:1-15	35	2:10	96
26:1-6	35	2:11	72, 98
31:31-34	104	2:13-14,22,41	123
Ezekiel		2:16	131
18:25	144	2:20,41	123
33:17	144	2:29-32	98
33:20	144	2:29-32,37	123
Daniel		2:32	112
7:13-14	184	2:39-40,51-52	88
Joel		2:49	92
3:1-5	124, 168	3:1-2	78
Jonah		3:4	146
4:10-11	114	3:6	73, 87, 112
Micah		3:14	75
3:12	35	3:16	144
Zechariah		3:21	126
8:20-23	35	3:21-22	20
Matthew		4:1	106
7:11	102	4:1-14	103
28:18	131	4:6-8	131
Mark		4:14-20	20
1:7	144	4:14-30	64
9:38	144	4:16-30	73, 123, 181
10:17,32	145	4:18	33
14:27,50	132	4:18-30	35
Luke		4:43	80
1	90, 94	5:1-11	140
1:2	23	5:14	123
1:3	11, 74	5:16	126
1:3-4	61	5:17-20	20
1:4	74	5:20	142
1:22	123	5:25-26	126
1:26-38	140	5:27-31	127
1:32	92	5:32	143
1:47-55,68-79	123	6:12	126
		6:12-16	131, 140
		6:13-16	80
		6:23	152
		6:27-38	152
		6:28	126

Scripture References

Luke (continued)		11:2	92
6:36	92	11:13	102, 147
7:1-10	75, 114	11:32	143
7:9	177	12:4	152
7:11-17	64	12:11-12	152
7:16	126	12:22-31	123
8:4-18	139	12:30	92
8:5-15	82	12:49	24, 81
8:11	82	13:3-5	143
8:12-15	142	13:13	126
8:15	82, 84	13:18-19	139
8:25	142	13:18-21	146
8:39	123	13:22,33	35
8:40-42,49-56	64	13:34	152
8:48-50	142	14	127
9:1-5	140	14:26-27	152
9:1-11	131	17:10	183
9:10-17	127	17:11-19	113
9:16	123	17:19	142
9:16-17	127	18:1-8	126, 147
9:18,28	126	18:8	142
9:23-26	152	18:42	142
9:31	97, 145	19:1-10	145
9:46-50	131	19:10	71
9:49	144	19:11	111
9:51	35	19:11-27	146
9:51-19:27	67, 94, 101, 139, 145	19:24-27	131
		19:46	123
9:51-62	146	20:21-26	75
9:54	96	20:42	97
9:57-62	146	21:12-13	181
10:1,38	35	21:36	126
10:1-16	80	22:8	123
10:1-20	140	22:14-20	127
10:2	126	22:15-38	127
10:2-13	147	22:18	111
10:21	92	22:24-27	131
10:21-22	123, 126	22:28	152
10:23-24	123	22:29	92
10:29-37	113, 145	22:32,41-45	126
11:1	126	22:41	126
11:1-13	126, 147	22:67	88

Scripture References

Luke (*continued*)

22:69	97
23:13-16	75
23:34	101, 185
23:34,46	92
23:34-36	64
23:35-38	88
23:42	111
23:47	75
24	127
24:13-35	65, 118
24:21	35
24:26	97, 111
24:30-31	123
24:30-35,41-43	127
24:30-53	99
24:32-35	125
24:35	128
24:44	131
24:46-48	129
24:46-49	154, 165
24:47	73, 143
24:47-48	68
24:48-49	112
24:50-51	96
24:50-53	124
24:52	39, 124

Acts of Apostles

1-12	67
1-15	67
1:1	74
1:1-2	9
1:1-11	170
1:2	105, 131
1:2,8	101
1:2,11,22	97
1:3	111
1:4	92
1:4-5	54, 93
1:5	102, 112, 149
1:6	35
1:6-11	99
1:7	92-93
1:7-8	87
1:8	33, 68, 73, 105-106, 112, 129, 150-151, 154, 172
1:12-14	132
1:13	16, 38
1:13-14	38
1:14	126, 178
1:14,24-25	39
1:15	179
1:15-17,20-26	178
1:15-26	38, 132
1:16	102-103
1:21	148
1:21-22	131
1:23	38
1:23-48	178
1:24	92
1:24-25	126
2:1	178
2:1-4	20, 55, 102, 112
2:1-11	172
2:1-13	141
2:1-21	112
2:1-36	64
2:4	103, 105, 151
2:5-11	78, 90
2:11	90, 93
2:14	38, 141
2:14,22-28	167
2:14,36-41	168
2:14-36	38, 132, 181
2:14-37	102
2:14-40	73
2:14-41	20, 64
2:16-21	90
2:17,22,39,43	111
2:17-18	146, 151
2:17-21	102, 167
2:21	38, 55

Scripture References

Acts of Apostles (*continued*)		3:6	55
2:21-36	111	3:6,16	100
2:22	90, 93, 95, 100	3:8	93
2:22-23	111	3:11-12	141
2:22-24,30-32	95	3:12-26	38, 132
2:23	91, 143	3:13	81, 95
2:24	97, 143	3:13,16	125
2:24,32	54, 91	3:13-14	143
2:25	156	3:13-15,17-19	174
2:25-28	145	3:14-15	88
2:31,36	98	3:15	95, 98, 101, 155
2:32	155	3:15,22,26	91
2:33	93, 98, 102	3:15,26	95
2:33,38	101	3:18	93
2:34	97	3:18-21	91
2:34-36	95	3:19	54
2:38	54-56, 100, 139, 142-144, 149, 151	3:20	90, 96
		3:20-21	114
2:38,47	144	3:22-23	98
2:38-39	102	3:25	111
2:39	111-112	3:26	96, 101
2:40	54	4:1,13	16
2:41	35, 37, 64, 149, 168	4:2,10	54
		4:3	152
2:41,47	117	4:4	144
2:42	56, 109, 126, 128, 166	4:7	154
		4:8	103, 105, 151
2:42-45	39	4:8,31	104
2:42-47	37-38, 55, 118-119, 166	4:8-12	38, 175
		4:10	91, 95, 100
2:43	54	4:10,30	55
2:43-47	64	4:10-11	143
2:44	142	4:11	96, 110
2:44-45	39, 120	4:12	38, 54-55, 72, 99, 100
2:46	120, 126, 128		
2:46-47	39, 155	4:13	149, 156
2:47	37, 54, 93, 111, 119	4:18	55, 100
		4:19	92
3:1	16, 126	4:19-20	154
3:1-10	20, 45, 64, 100, 132, 141	4:20	39, 148, 156
		4:21	93
3:2-10	64	4:23-26	124

Scripture References

Acts of Apostles (*continued*)		5:28,40	100
4:23-31	37	5:29	84
4:24	91	5:29-32	38, 55
4:24-30	55, 126	5:30	95
4:25	57, 102-103	5:30-32	161
4:27	95-96	5:31	95, 98-99, 101, 143
4:28	91	5:32	54, 57, 103-104
4:29	83, 85, 152	5:39	90
4:29-30	157	5:40	152
4:30	96, 100, 125	5:41	55, 100, 123, 152
4:31	103, 126, 150-151, 156	5:41-42	39
4:32	39, 117, 120, 142	5:42	55, 84, 125, 156
4:32-35	37, 39, 55-56, 118-119, 173	6:1-2	134
		6:1-6	38-39, 133, 156
4:32-37	64	6:1-7	103, 168
4:33	91, 100, 143, 180	6:2	83
4:34	66, 120	6:2-4	84
4:35	119	6:2-6	132
4:37	120, 134	6:3	105, 151, 156
5:1-11	37-38, 121, 132	6:3-6	132
5:3	55, 57, 106	6:4	126, 147
5:3,32	151	6:5	103, 105, 151
5:3,9	103	6:7	39, 57, 68, 81-83, 91, 142, 144, 155
5:11	111, 125		
5:12	125	6:8	106
5:12-13,42	38	6:10	91, 103
5:12-14	54	7:1-53	40
5:12-16	64, 179	7:2	91
5:13	55	7:2-53	90
5:13-14	39	7:32-34	91
5:14	37, 117, 142, 180	7:37	98, 111
5:14-16	132	7:51	104, 106
5:15	64, 66	7:51-53	150
5:15-16	20, 64, 125	7:52	152
5:16	64	7:54-56	101
5:17-18	37, 181	7:55	103, 151
5:17-21	38, 132	7:55-56	97
5:19	91, 101	7:55-60	40, 184
5:19-21	125	7:56	98-99, 184-185
5:20	84	7:58-60	152
5:27-32,40-41	180	7:59	127
5:28	55	7:59-60	64

Scripture References

Acts of Apostles (*continued*)		9:1-16,27	101
7:60	101, 185	9:1-18	65
8:1	40, 134, 152	9:1-19	132
8:1,3	111	9:1-25	42
8:1,4	99	9:2	143, 145, 148
8:1-3	121	9:3-9	141
8:1-5	122	9:4	56, 99, 148
8:4	82, 154	9:6,10	131
8:4-13	40	9:10	42
8:4-24	102	9:10-16	141, 148
8:4-6	84	9:10-19	134
8:5	98	9:11	127
8:5-8,14-17	170	9:14,21	55
8:8,39	41, 64	9:15	72
8:9-24	44, 64	9:15,27	100
8:10	89	9:15,28	55
8:12	55, 100, 149	9:16	55, 101, 152, 176
8:14	119	9:17	103
8:14-15	149	9:17-19	102
8:14-17	41, 55, 112	9:20	98, 181
8:14-17,25	16	9:21	153
8:14-25	113	9:22,44	22
8:15	127	9:26	97, 153
8:16	55, 100	9:26-28	122
8:17	105	9:26-31	176
8:18-24	64	9:30	42, 181
8:20-22	106, 143	9:31	41, 54, 64, 68, 103, 105, 111-112, 119, 151
8:22	127		
8:24	148		
8:25	125, 155	9:32-35	20
8:26	54, 91	9:32-42	132
8:26,39	41	9:33-35	64
8:26-40	65, 102	9:34	100
8:29	105, 146	9:35,42	143
8:29,39	103	9:36	134
8:29-39	103	9:36-43	64
8:30-31	81	9:40	127, 148
8:32	152	9:42	142, 144
8:32-35	96	10-11	114
8:35	131	10:1-8	141
8:39	150	10:1-23	54
9:1-2	37	10:1-48	114

Scripture References

Acts of Apostles (*continued*)

Reference	Pages
10:1-11:18	39, 132
10:2	134
10:3	91
10:9	126
10:9-15	148
10:9-16	125
10:9-16,23-48	65
10:9-23	141, 178
10:9-48	38, 132
10:15	92
10:17-21	103
10:19	103, 105, 146, 150
10:25	125
10:25-26,34-35,44-48	177
10:31	92
10:34	92
10:34,37-43	165
10:34-35	113, 147
10:34-43	38, 132
10:36	98
10:37-38	106
10:37-43	96
10:38	33, 80, 95, 150
10:38-39	94, 95
10:39	155
10:40	91
10:41	127
10:42	91, 95, 99, 155
10:42-43	144
10:43	55, 72, 100, 142-143
10:44	55, 112, 146
10:44-48	57, 102
10:47	149
10:48	55, 100
11:1	83
11:1-4	132
11:1-18	65, 132, 177-178
11:1-19	65
11:5	148
11:9	114
11:12	103, 146, 150
11:14	117
11:16-17	149
11:17	103, 142
11:17-18	92-93
11:18	56, 68, 72, 125
11:18-19	40
11:19	42, 134, 152
11:19-21	130, 154
11:19-26	122
11:21,24	143
11:21-24	144
11:22,26	111
11:24	103, 105, 142, 151
11:25-26	181
11:25-26,30	42
11:27-29	133-134
11:28	103, 105
11:28-29	119, 153
11:28-30	57
12:1-2	152
12:1-19	121
12:2-17	121
12:5,12	126
12:6-11	39, 132
12:7	54, 91, 101
12:12	120, 126, 134, 148
12:17	39, 92
12:24	57, 68, 81-83, 91, 155
12:24-25	42
12:36-38	97
13-28	67
13:1	130-131, 134
13:1-3	57, 119, 133, 155, 183
13:1-5	150
13:1-14:28	43
13:2	103, 124
13:2-3	44, 126, 128, 148
13:4	103, 105, 146, 150
13:5,46-49	91
13:6-11	64

Scripture References

Acts of Apostles (*continued*)		14:27	45, 72, 92-93
13:6-12	44, 64	14:27-28	118, 120
13:7,12	76	14:28	68
13:9	103, 105-106, 151	15	114
13:11	91	15-28	67
13:13	46	15:1	133
13:14	124	15:1-2	121
13:14,43-52	181	15:1-2,22-29	183
13:15-52	73	15:1-3	56
13:16	141	15:1-35	78
13:16-41	20, 64	15:2	122, 132
13:23	95, 98	15:2-29	132
13:25	146	15:3,12	73
13:30,34,37	91	15:4	118, 120
13:33	98	15:6,22-23	132
13:38	99, 143	15:6-29	56
13:39	142	15:7-11	38, 132, 184
13:45	122	15:8	151
13:45-46	88	15:9	142
13:46	183	15:11	141-142
13:46-47	45	15:12	54
13:46-48	72	15:13-21	133
13:46-52	103	15:14	92
13:47	98	15:14-18	114
13:48	57, 81, 141-142, 144	15:22	46, 119, 132
13:48,52	64	15:22,32	134
13:52	103, 105, 151	15:22-29	46
14:1,21	144	15:23	132
14:3	95, 141, 143, 155-157	15:23-29	73
14:5	122	15:24	153
14:6-7	156	15:26	101
14:8-10	20, 64	15:28	57, 103-104, 151, 184
14:11-12	89	15:29	184
14:11-13	125	15:30-33	118, 120
14:14-15	153	15:32	157
14:15	91	15:35	155
14:19	153	15:36	120
14:21-23	118	15:36-41	134
14:21-27	182	15:37-39	122
14:22	142, 153	15:39	46
14:23	127, 133, 142, 148	15:41	46
14:25-27	92	16	55

Scripture References

Acts of Apostles (*continued*)		18:5	155
16:1,10	12	18:6	73
16:2-3	134	18:8	97, 142
16:4	46	18:9-10	154
16:5	68, 119, 142	18:9-11	153
16:6	57	18:11	91
16:6-10	146	18:12-16	76
16:6-7	101, 103, 105, 150	18:22	120
16:7	55, 98, 106	18:23	49
16:9	54	18:24-26	150
16:10	13	18:24-28	134
16:13	127, 148	18:25-26	143, 145
16:14	141, 143	18:27	142
16:14-15	118	18:31-32	22
16:14-16	134	19:1-7	102
16:16,25	127	19:2	142, 150
16:17	91	19:5	55, 68, 100
16:18	55, 64, 100	19:6	55, 105, 112, 146, 151
16:22	153		
16:25-34	125	19:8	49
16:30-31	117	19:9	49
16:31	72, 142	19:9,23	143, 145
16:32	142	19:9-11	153
16:34	64, 118, 127	19:10,17,20	49
16:37	76	19:11	54, 91
16:40	118, 120	19:11-12	20, 64
17:3	98	19:12	64
17:16	48	19:17	55
17:16-34	146	19:20	55, 57, 81
17:22-31	66	19:21	105
17:22-34	48	19:21-22	49
17:24	91	19:28-41	153
17:24,29	89	20:2-3	49
17:24-31	93	20:7	124
17:26	91	20:7-11	126, 128
17:27	90	20:9-10	64
17:30	90	20:19	152
17:30-31	144	20:21	142
17:31	91, 95	20:22	146, 150
17:34	142, 144	20:22-23	22, 51, 103, 105
18:1-4	134	20:23	55, 151
18:2	134	20:24	80, 131, 146

Scripture References

Acts of Apostles (*continued*)			
20:24,32	95	23:23-25	76
20:27	87, 91	24:14,22	145
20:28	55, 101, 105	24:17	120, 134
20:28-31	157	24:18	124
20:29-30	122	24:24	142
20:29-31	153	24:26	52
20:36	126-127	25:27	52
20:36-38	148	26:8	91
21:4	103, 150	26:9-18	132
21:4,11	103, 105	26:12-18	65, 101
21:4-5,11	22	26:16	155
21:4-6	57	26:18	142-143
21:5	126	26:22	155-156
21:7-14	120	26:29	127
21:7-14,17-25	118	26:31-32	76
21:9-11	134	26:32	52
21:10-11	57	27:1	53
21:11	105	27:1-28:15	66
21:13	55, 100, 152	27:1-28:16	76, 101
21:13-14	153	27:3	53
21:14	153	27:23	91
21:18	39, 133	27:34-36	129
21:19	55, 73	27:35	128
21:20	55	28:8	127, 147
21:20-21	122, 153	28:15	118, 157
21:20-24	51	28:16	76, 154
21:27	97	28:16-31	146
21:27-30	122	28:20	153
22:3-21	132	28:23	127
22:4	145	28:23-28	103
22:6-16	65	28:25	102-103
22:6-16,17-21	101	28:26-27	153
22:14-15	98	28:28	56, 73, 93, 98
22:16	55, 72, 100	28:31	64
22:17	127	**Romans**	
22:19	142	16:25	26
22:21	165	**2 Corinthians**	
22:25	76	8:18	12
22:26	76	**Galatians**	
23:11	101, 146, 154, 157	1:17	43
23:16-30	76		

Scripture References

Galatians (*continued*)
1:19	172
2:11-14	121, 183
2:13	46

Ephesians
2:13	165

Colossians
4:14	12, 75

2 Timothy
4:11	12

Philemon
24	12

Hebrews
9:3	34

1 Peter
3:15	156

Index of Authors Cited

Achtemeier, P. J. 121
Barnabas (Epistle of) 174
Betz, O. 82
Brown, S. 117
Bruce, F. F. 13, 104
Caird, G. B. 75, 95
Cassidy, R. 40
Conzelmann, H. 71, 75
Didache 174
Doohan, H. 15
Doohan, L. 28
Franklin, E. 77, 106
Goodenough, E. R. 75
Hengel, M. 111
Hultgren, A. 77, 129
Irenaeus 16
Juel, D. 62, 113
Kodell, J. 81, 119
Lampe, G. W. H. 94

Leaney, A. R. C. 75
MacRae, G. 93
Marshall, I. H. 71-72, 98, 106, 116
Minear, P. S. 82, 84
Munck, J. 75
Navone, J. 105, 127, 151
O'Neill, J. C. 62
Pathrapankal, J. 122
Pervo, R. I. 131
Praeder, S. M. 67
Robinson, W. C. 83
Scharper, P. 40
Tertullian 16
van Stempvoort, P. A. 116
van Unnik, W. C. 27
Walaskay, P. 76, 117, 127

Index of Subjects

Acts of Apostles, as a form of literature 16-17
adult education vii, ix
Antioch 13, 18-19, 24, 42-43, 45-46, 49, 67-68, 70, 72, 78, 88, 118, 121, 126, 128-130, 133, 150, 157, 181-183
apostle(s) 4, 9, 11-12, 15-17, 33-34, 36-38, 41, 45-46, 56, 59, 65, 68-69, 72-73, 80-81, 84, 88-89, 91-92, 97-101, 103-105, 109, 118, 120, 125, 127-129, 131-134, 165-166, 170-172, 174, 178-181, 183-184
authority 3, 10-11, 13, 26, 38, 55, 78, 115, 127, 131-133
baptism 38, 41, 55-56, 67, 69, 102, 144, 149-150, 159, 162, 168, 170, 173, 177-178, 184
  of Jesus 20, 33, 94
  of the Church 20, 33-34
Barnabas 16, 42-46, 56-57, 70, 72, 80, 88-89, 105, 120-122, 127, 129, 133-134, 136, 150-151, 156, 182-183
blessing(s) 38, 56, 92-93
boldness 34, 37, 57, 83, 85, 88, 103, 126, 148, 151, 156-157, 160
Breaking of Bread 50, 56, 100, 109, 118-119, 124, 127-129, 140, 166
Bruce, F. F. 28
Bultmann, Rudolf 27, 115
call 30, 141, 158, 167, 175
  God's 37, 126, 182-183
  Jesus' original ix, 24, 29, 57, 79, 139
  Luke's 3, 7, 80, 130, 159
  of Paul 65
  to conversion 5, 115, 143, 182
  to discipleship 140-141,

Index of Subjects

call *(continued)*
   145, 149, 158-159
  to ministry 1, 29, 69,
   80-81, 84, 129-130
  to repentance 175
canon of Sacred Scripture
  9, 17, 23
catechist(s) 12
celebration 148, 158-159
celebration(s) 5-7, 37, 50,
  56, 123-124, 128-129, 135,
  163-165, 167
charism(s) 2, 25
charity 174, 182
Chosen People 7, 35, 97,
  117, 132, 171-173, 178
christology 145
  Luke's 15, 93-94
Church vii-xiii, 1-7, 15-17,
  20, 22-27, 29-30, 33-35,
  38-40, 42-43, 45, 50-51,
  54-62, 64, 66, 68-74,
  76-81, 83-87, 91-110,
  112-122, 124-125,
  128-136, 139-142,
  144-152, 154-163,
  165-180, 182-185, 188
  as the people of God 7, 55,
   81, 111, 113, 132
  birth of 38, 68-69, 102,
   112, 124, 172-173
  contemporary viii
  enthusiasm of early 2, 5,
   7, 57
  expansion of 12, 33, 35,
   37, 40-42, 54, 58, 64, 68,
   76, 82-83, 122, 187
  history of 1, 11, 21, 62, 82,
   106, 110
  in crises 109, 122
  Luke's description of
   early vii-viii, 24, 64, 66,
   109-113, 115, 117, 119,
   121-123, 125-127, 129,
   131-135, 137, 173-174, 188
  Luke's vision of 4, 12, 19,
   23, 65, 78, 85, 110-111,
   161, 172, 178, 187
  structures of 6, 9, 11, 15,
   24, 27, 38
  understanding of 41, 188
  universality of 6, 58,
   112-115, 170-171, 173
Church leaders 5, 11-13, 15,
  26, 34, 38-39, 41, 51, 57,
  76, 80, 83, 100, 105, 114,
  117-118, 122, 126, 129,
  132, 137, 169-170, 184
collegiality 1, 3, 132-133
community 1-7, ix-xi, 29,
  31, 33, 37-40, 42-45,
  47-48, 50-51, 53-59, 69,
  74, 78, 81-84, 86, 98,
  100-104, 108-112,
  114-115, 117-124,
  126-128, 131-136, 140,
  142, 149, 152-153, 155,
  157-158, 160-161,
  164-174, 179-180, 183, 188
  and sharing 4, 6, 10-11, 37,
   39, 55-56, 118-120, 122,
   127-129, 134, 136, 140,
   142, 158, 165-166, 171,
   174, 178, 184, 187-188
  Luke's 4, viii, 15, 21, 28,
   62, 77, 116, 130, 161, 171
  Luke's vision of 4, 6
compassion 10, 90-95, 101,
  143, 157
conversion 5, 39, 41, 45, 65,
  72-73, 82, 115, 118-119,
  141-144, 146, 149,
  158-159, 167-168, 174, 177

Index of Subjects

conversion (*continued*)
  of Paul 42-44, 51, 72, 127, 176
Conzelmann, Hans 28
Cornelius 19, 42, 44, 65, 72, 80, 91, 112, 114, 134, 141, 149, 165, 177-178, 184
covenant 34, 111-112
deacon(s) 16, 38-40, 51, 80-81, 97, 105, 126, 129, 133-134, 151, 169, 176
detachment 141, 159
dialogue 66, 77, 79, 82, 114, 118, 122
  between Church and civil institutions 5, 24, 74, 76, 78, 85
  between Jews and Gentiles 78
  between Judaism and Christianity 77, 113, 121
  between religion and society 83
Dibelius, Martin 27
discernment 2, 25, 29, 43, 57, 103, 126-127, 148, 169, 179, 184
disciple(s) 20, 29, 34-35, 37, 39, 45-46, 54, 57, 69, 80, 135, 140-143, 145-160, 166, 168, 171, 176-178, 180, 182, 188
discipleship viii, 67, 135, 139-141, 144-146, 157-159
divine plan 54, 73, 91-92, 95, 107, 110, 124
"early Catholicism" 9, 27, 115
Easter viii-ix, 31, 158, 160-161, 163-168, 170-171, 173-184, 188
ecclesiology 127, 145

elders 34, 38, 46, 50-51, 78-79, 87, 127, 133-134, 148, 150, 175-176, 183-185
empire 1, 23-24, 43, 68, 74-76, 78-79
enthusiasm 62, 118-120, 125, 131
eschatology 15, 98, 102, 111, 115-117, 119, 129
Eucharist 11, 108, 128-129, 135, 162-163
evangelization 4, 6-7, 10, 12, 15, 34-35, 40, 57-59, 66, 72, 83-84, 87, 91, 99, 103-104, 106, 119, 125, 127, 145, 158, 165, 168-171, 177-178, 183, 187
exodus 144
  from Egypt 97
  Jesus' 97, 145
  the Church's 146
faith 1-7, viii-xi, 17, 22, 24-27, 29-31, 39, 45-46, 48, 54, 56-58, 72, 75, 77, 79-83, 86, 94, 96-98, 101, 104, 107-110, 113, 115-116, 118-120, 128-129, 141-144, 146, 148-152, 154, 158-159, 161-171, 173-174, 176-177, 179-180, 182-183, 185, 187
  Luke's 2, 25
  origins of ix, 22
Fitzmyer, Joseph 28
forgiveness 55, 99-101, 124, 127, 141-144, 151, 161, 168, 174-175, 181, 185
Gentile(s) 2, 5, 11, 14-15, 20, 23, 39-40, 42-46, 51, 55-56, 60, 63-67, 72-73, 77-79, 83-84, 88-89, 92,

Index of Subjects

Gentile(s) (*continued*)
    95, 103-104, 112-115, 121, 125, 132-133, 165, 168, 173, 177-178, 181-184
Gospels
  as a form of literature 15
  shared sources in 18, 27
Haenchen, Ernst 28
hierarchy 10
Holy Spirit 7, 33-35, 38, 41-46, 51, 54-58, 68-69, 80, 84-85, 87, 90, 92-93, 97-99, 101-108, 111-113, 116, 124, 127, 131, 139, 142, 144, 146-147, 149-151, 153, 156, 158-159, 161, 165-166, 168, 170-173, 175, 177, 181, 184-185, 187-188
hope 12, 56, 62, 141, 156-158, 188
Hort, F. J. A. 27
hospitality 118, 134
Ignatius of Antioch 17, 24
imposition of hands 11, 41, 44, 59, 127
initiation, in early Church 45
inspiration 25, 57, 101-103, 105, 150
James 19, 23, 25, 39, 78, 121-122, 133, 152
  as leader 16, 184
Jerusalem 10, 19, 23, 33-35, 37-43, 45-46, 48, 51, 56, 67-69, 73, 76, 78-80, 82-83, 87, 94, 96, 102, 112-114, 118, 120-122, 126, 129, 133, 145-149, 153-155, 159, 165, 167-168, 170, 172-173, 177, 181, 183

Jerusalem Church 16, 43, 45-46, 51, 120-122, 126, 134, 152, 172, 184
Jerusalem Council 19, 43, 46, 72, 78, 103, 114, 132-134, 151, 153, 156, 184
Jesus
  as leader 98-99, 161
  as servant 96-97, 101, 106, 125, 154, 174
  as Son of Man 71, 97-99, 184-185
  ascension of 19, 34, 38, 96, 99, 104, 108, 112, 124, 154, 168, 170-171
  cross of 75, 88, 130
  crucifixion of 165, 175
  name of 7, 38-39, 44, 54-55, 72, 95-96, 99-102, 108, 123-125, 127, 139-141, 143, 149, 152, 166, 168, 175-176, 180, 185
  passion of 51, 97, 111, 116, 145
  resurrection of 7, 33, 54, 91, 94-95, 97, 99-100, 107, 164-165, 178-180
Jewish leaders 35-38, 70, 74, 88, 113, 121, 148, 156
John 3, 9, 36-37, 41, 61, 82, 102, 126, 149, 152, 156, 170
journey(s) 4, 6, 10, 65, 67-68, 70, 85, 114, 118, 129, 140-141, 143-148, 158
  Jesus' 35, 51, 67, 79-80, 126, 129, 139, 144-146, 159
  Paul's 13-14, 26, 43-49, 51, 53, 66-67, 72-73, 78, 80,

Index of Subjects

journey(s) *(continued)* 126, 128, 132, 145, 182-183
  Peter's 41, 145
  Philip's 40-41, 145
  spiritual 4, 145
joy 5, 10, 39, 41, 57, 64, 96, 105, 119, 145, 151, 162, 170
Judaism 15, 41-42, 45, 55-56, 89, 97, 100, 111-115, 121, 123-124, 168, 172, 177-178, 182-183
Käsemann, Ernst 27
kerygma 82, 97, 162, 166
kingdom of God 33, 35, 95, 111
Kümmel, W. G. 67
Last Supper 128
leadership 23-25, 39, 59, 131-133, 137, 165, 169, 171-172, 178, 181, 184-185
Lightfoot, J. B. 27
liturgical year 10, 29
liturgy 6, 28, 124, 128
Lord's Supper 37
love 5, 62, 173
Luke
  as catechist 1, 29, 188
  as pastoral leader 1-2
  as author of Acts 2, 9-14, 20, 24-26, 61-63, 187
  as evangelist 10, 72, 99, 101, 161
  as historian vii, 2, 21-29, 31, 77, 82, 113, 115-117, 161, 187
  as pastoral leader viii, 24-25, 29, 31, 62-63, 72, 76-77, 79, 83, 116, 187
  as storyteller 62
  as theologian 2, 12, 18, 20-25, 27-31, 62-63, 71, 82, 117, 161, 187
  as writer 2, 9, 11, 14-21, 27, 61-68, 71, 74-78, 80-81, 83-85
  enthusiasm of viii-x, 2, 12, 24, 31, 187
Marcion 23
Mark 3, 15, 18-19, 23, 25, 35, 43, 46, 57, 61-63, 66, 80, 82, 113, 122, 132, 136, 140, 145
Marshall, I. Howard 28
Mary 16, 65, 171-172
Matthew 3, 18, 61, 63, 101, 131, 140
Messiah 39, 44, 96, 98, 102, 125, 168, 174
minister(s) viii, 11, 23, 29-30, 51, 54, 58-59, 85, 91, 101, 103, 106-108, 118, 129-131, 133-134, 141-142, 146-147
  pastoral vii
ministry vi-vii, 1-3, 10-11, 15-16, 24, 29, 34-35, 46, 49, 58-59, 64, 67-73, 77-81, 83-84, 91-103, 105-106, 109, 112, 114, 116, 118-119, 122, 126-127, 129-133, 136, 140-141, 143, 147, 151-153, 155, 158-159, 165, 167-169, 171, 176, 179, 183, 187-188
miracle(s) 36-37, 40, 42, 53-55, 89, 91, 100-101, 125, 127, 132, 167, 170, 174-175, 180-181
mission vii-viii, 30, 33, 39, 41, 44-45, 51, 56-57, 67, 71, 73, 77, 83, 86-87, 92,

Index of Subjects

mission (*continued*) 94, 96, 99, 103, 112-116, 118, 125, 132-133, 140-141, 145-146, 148, 154-158, 165, 170-171, 176-177, 188
missionaries 5, 12-13, 42, 45-46, 50, 56, 58-59, 89, 91, 105, 114, 118-119, 133-135, 143, 146-148, 182, 185
mystagogia ix, 162-164
obedience 39, 57, 95, 103
Paul 12-20, 22, 25-27, 30, 42-54, 56-57, 59, 64-67, 70, 72-73, 75-76, 78, 80, 82, 87-91, 99, 102, 114, 120-122, 125-129, 131-134, 136, 145-146, 148, 150, 152-157, 176-178, 181-183
 as leader 23, 105, 132, 185
 co-workers of 49-51, 78, 127, 132, 134, 145, 182
peace 41, 54, 170, 173, 177
Pentecost 10, 19, 34, 37-38, 45, 78, 88, 90, 96-97, 102-103, 111-112, 116, 124, 145, 163-164, 166-167, 170, 172, 178-179, 181, 185
persecution 3, 6, 17, 34, 37, 39-40, 45, 51, 58, 69, 82, 84, 99, 121-122, 134-135, 151-155, 158, 160, 176-177, 183, 185, 188
perseverance 142, 147, 151, 154
Peter 16-17, 19-20, 22, 25, 27, 35-37, 39, 41-42, 44-46, 56, 64-66, 69-70, 73, 78-80, 88, 90-91, 94, 96-97, 100, 102, 105, 111-112, 114, 121-122, 124-127, 129, 132-133, 136, 141, 145, 148-149, 152, 156, 165-168, 170, 172, 174-181, 184
 as leader 4, 38-39, 126, 132, 178
Pharisaic Judaism 3
Pharisee(s) 48, 52, 74, 89, 113
Philemon 12
Philip 16-17, 19, 25, 39-41, 51, 91, 96, 102, 113, 125, 141, 145, 150, 170
Polycarp 18, 24
poor 78, 95, 102, 135, 156
poverty 119
praise 57, 72, 93, 123, 127, 147
prayer(s) 6, 11, 34, 43, 56, 58, 70, 86, 92, 109, 118-119, 123, 126-130, 135, 137, 140, 147-148, 158-159, 166, 171-172, 179, 188
preaching 6, 34, 36-37, 41, 43, 50, 54, 88, 92, 95, 99-100, 103-104, 106, 108, 110-112, 125, 130, 134, 167, 174-175, 182
proclamation 6, 29, 69, 83, 87, 89, 98, 103, 115, 125, 162, 169, 182, 187
prophecy 105, 151
prophet(s) 35, 57, 91, 96, 98, 107, 111, 131, 133-135, 152-153
Ramsay, W. M. 27
renewal 2-4, vii-ix, 24, 67, 80, 130, 135, 158
 Luke's vision of 3

Index of Subjects

repentance 7, 38, 54, 56, 72, 90, 92, 115, 139, 143, 149, 161, 164-168, 175, 181-182
responsibility 1, 7, 12, 22, 25, 29-30, 58-59, 62, 83, 102, 126, 130, 132, 143, 155, 157-158, 165, 171, 178, 180-182, 184
revelation 6, 87, 89-90, 106, 112
Rite of Christian Initiation of Adults ix
ritual(s) 6, 11, 26, 56, 123-124, 128-129, 135, 137
Rome 12-13, 17, 48, 51, 53-54, 56, 67-68, 70, 73-76, 78, 80, 83, 128, 146, 148, 154, 157, 177
sacraments 10
Sadducee(s) 52, 74, 113
salvation 22, 35, 38, 55-56, 71-73, 83, 87-88, 92, 95-96, 110, 112, 114-117, 129, 132, 141-142, 144-145, 168, 175-176
 universal 72, 79, 83, 93, 112, 116-117, 146, 187
salvation history 71, 77, 82, 90-91, 98, 113, 115-117, 124, 156, 171
Samaria 33, 40-42, 56, 68-69, 87, 112, 126, 152, 177
Samaritan(s) 5, 40-41, 60, 73, 79, 95-96, 113, 115, 145, 149, 170, 177
second coming 27, 71, 77, 97, 109, 171
service 3
 Luke's 2
Silas 16, 46, 48, 57, 127, 133, 157

sin 55, 99-100, 139, 142-144, 149, 161, 167-168, 174
social justice 1, 24
sources, Luke's use of 11, 18-21, 24-25, 29, 63, 65, 76, 113, 131-132, 144-145
speech(es) 19-20, 65-67, 73
 Jesus' 20, 73
 Paul's 48, 51, 66, 73, 89
 Peter's 20, 73
 Stephen 16, 19, 39-40, 69, 79, 90, 97, 99, 105, 113, 121, 127, 151-152, 184-185
Streeter, B. H. 27
suffering 34, 39, 55, 59, 96, 100-101, 121-123, 135, 151-154, 158, 175-176, 183
Temple 34-37, 39, 51, 55, 113, 120, 123-127, 167, 180
Timothy 12, 46, 48, 57, 80, 133
tradition(s) 9-12, 19, 21-23, 25-27, 29-30, 85
 Jewish 2, 20
 oral 1, 25, 28
 Palestinian 11
Twelve, the 16-17, 38-39, 65, 69, 80, 103, 129-132, 158, 169, 171-172, 178-179, 185
union/unity 37, 78-79, 97, 102, 104, 117-119, 122, 135-136, 147-148, 158, 169, 172-174, 176, 188
universal call to holiness 1-2, 6, 29, 158
Vatican Council II 158
vision(s) 5, ix, 24, 53-54, 100-101, 125, 146, 151, 157-158, 169
 Church leaders' 5
 community's 55, 57, 121

Index of Subjects

vision(s) (*continued*)
  disciples' 35, 46, 90, 104, 158
  Jesus' 81, 146-147
  Luke's 3-4, 6, viii, 10, 12, 19-20, 23, 29, 62, 65, 78, 80-81, 110, 113, 172, 187-188
  Paul's 25, 45, 125, 148
  Peter's 42, 114, 125, 177, 184
  Philip's 125
  Stephen's 185
  the Church's 114
Way, the 7, 84, 117, 124, 141, 143-151, 153-154, 158-159
"we passages" 13-14
Wescott, B. F. 27

witness(es) 2, 7, 16, 23, 33, 38, 42, 62, 68, 82, 87, 90, 93-95, 100, 103-106, 112, 119, 131-132, 143, 146, 148-150, 154-159, 161, 165-166, 171, 173, 178-182, 184, 188
Word, the 2, 6, 12, 23-24, 29-30, 34, 37, 39, 41-42, 55, 57-59, 71-72, 79, 81-86, 88, 92, 99, 103, 108, 120, 124-126, 128, 131-134, 142, 144, 148, 155, 160, 168-170, 173-174, 177, 182-185, 187-188
worship 6, 119, 123-125, 127-128, 167, 188

How to Use *Acts of Apostles* to Build Faith Communities

Now that you've read *Acts of Apostles*, how can you share it with other members of your community? Using the companion *Leader's Guide*, pastoral leaders can invoke the early Church's spirit of faith-sharing in today's parish groups. Outlines, focus questions, discussion topics, and practical suggestions will help communities develop spiritually, liturgically, and pastorally.

Acts of Apostles is tailored for faith-sharing in small communities and parish core groups, including:

- bible study groups
- adult initiation groups
- liturgy planning teams
- outreach groups

The author outlines the stages of group development, then compares these with the stages of life in the Church. He offers tips for preparation, necessary materials, meeting space, guidance, and group process. Each session follows the corresponding chapter in *Acts of Apostles* and includes a stated purpose, preparation, readings, discussion topics, questions, sharing, and leader's self-evaluation.

LEADER'S GUIDE TO *ACTS OF APOSTLES*
Leonard Doohan, PhD

Paper, 32 pages, $6.95, 5½" x 8½"
ISBN 0-89390-300-0

Order from your local bookstore, or use the order form on the last page.

SCRIPTURE FOR WORSHIP & EDUCATION
Books by Leonard Doohan

ACTS OF APOSTLES
Building Faith Communities
Paper, 240 pages, $14.95, 5½" x 8½"
ISBN 0-89390-292-6

MATTHEW
Spirituality for the 80s and 90s
Paper, 200 pages, $10.95, 5½" x 8½"
ISBN 0-89390-292-6

MARK
Visionary of Early Christianity
Paper, 192 pages, $10.95, 5½" x 8½"
ISBN 0-89390-261-6

LUKE
The Perennial Spirituality
Paper, 228 pages, $10.95, 5½" x 8½"
ISBN 0-89390-262-4

JOHN
Gospel for a New Age
Paper, 228 pages, $10.95, 5½" x 8½"
ISBN 0-89390-263-2

Set of all five titles: $54

Set of four Gospel titles: $40

The titles in the SCRIPTURE FOR WORSHIP series are written especially for pastoral ministers. Unlike exegetical commentaries, which provide verse-by-verse analysis, these provide a broader examination of the context and themes of the biblical books. Study the biblical book's author, his community, theology, and purpose in writing.

Order from your local bookstore, or use the order form on the last page.

Other Small-Group Resources

Everything You Need for a Moms' Spirituality Group

MOMS: DEVELOPING A MINISTRY
Paula Hagen & Patricia Hoyt

Paper, 176 pages, $19.95, 8½" x 11"
ISBN 0-89390-228-4

Everything you need to know about starting a Ministry of Mothers Sharing (MOMS) in your community: budgeting and staffing information, session outlines, prayer rituals, photocopiable evaluations and other forms.

MOMS FACILITATOR'S GUIDE
Paula Hagen, Vickie LoPiccolo Jennett, & Patricia Hoyt

Paper, 144 pages, $11.95, 8½" x 11"
ISBN 0-89390-256-X

The essential resource for the MOMS group leader includes the session outlines, prayer rituals and corresponding pages from the *Personal Journal*.

MOMS: A PERSONAL JOURNAL
Paula Hagen with Vickie LoPiccolo Jennett

Paper, 112 pages, $19.95, 7" x 10"
ISBN 0-89390-224-1

The group participant's edition includes discussion about self-esteem and self-acceptance, stress management, spirituality, friendship, feelings, and personal growth.

A PRAYER COMPANION FOR MOMS
Vickie LoPiccolo Jennett with Paula Hagen

Paper, 104 pages, $6.95, 4" x 6"
ISBN 0-89390-265-9

Ideal as a participant's gift for "continuing the journey," this small book helps women stay in touch with their spirituality, even in the most hectic moments.

Order from your local bookstore, or use the order form on the last page.

More Small-Group Resources

EUCHARIST!
An Eight-Session Ritual-Catechesis Experience for Adults
Susan S. Jorgensen

Paper, 208 pages, $29.95, 8½" x 11"
ISBN 0-89390-293-4

Group members work through the prayers of the Eucharist, from the opening rite to dismissal, and emerge with a deep understanding of the ritual words and gestures.

STORIES FOR CHRISTIAN INITIATION
Joseph J. Juknialis

Paper, 152 pages, $8.95, 5½" x 8½"
ISBN 0-89390-235-7

Organized around the catechumenate, each story includes lectionary passages, reflections, questions and rituals for group faith-sharing.

STORIES TO INVITE FAITH-SHARING
Experiencing the Lord through the Seasons
Mary McEntee McGill

Paper, 128 pages, $8.95, 5½" x 8½"
ISBN 0-89390-230-6

Based on real-life experiences, these stories can help group members recognize God's presence in everyday activities. Includes reflections, questions, Scripture Index and Theme Index.

Order Form

Order these resources from your local bookstore, or mail this form to:

Resource Publications, Inc.
160 E. Virginia Street #290 - WA
San Jose, CA 95112-5876
(408) 286-8505
(408) 287-8748 FAX

QTY	TITLE	PRICE	TOTAL

Subtotal: _____
CA residents add 7¼% sales tax
(Santa Clara Co. residents, 8¼%): _____
Postage and handling
($2 for order up to $20; 10% of order over $20 but less than $150; $15 for order of $150 or more): _____
Total: _____

☐ My check or money order is enclosed.
☐ Charge my ☐ Visa ☐ MC.
Expiration Date _____
Card # _____ - _____ - _____ - _____
Signature _____
Name (print) _____
Institution _____
Street _____
City/State/ZIP _____